Third Edition

Pamelyn Smythscott, M.Ed.

Education Consultant, Learning Coach, and

Certified "Big Pencil" Writing Specialist

ISBN 978-1-957781-40-2 (softcover)
ISBN 978-1-957781-41-9 (hardcover)
ISBN 978-1-957781-42-6 (ebook)
Library of Congress Control Number: 2022903550

Printed in the United States of America.

Book Vine Press
2516 Highland Dr.
Palatine, IL 60067

This guidebook was developed for:

Academic Coaches	Event Planners
Adjuncts	Executive Directors
Administrative Assistants	Fast Food Managers & Staff
Adult Learners	Foreign Exchange Students
Athletic Directors	Foster Parents
Athletes	Guidance Counselors
Baby Sitters	Healthcare Professionals
Book Clubs	Home Schoolers
Campus Directors	Hospital Staff
Caretakers	Human Resources
Church Administrators	International Program Managers
College & Career Specialists	Instructional Coaches & Strategists
College Professors	Landscapers
Computer Technicians	Librarians
Corporate Managers	Learning Coaches
Custodians	Medical Staff
Customer Service Staff	Military Staff
Curriculum Directors	New Employees
Day Care Providers	Nurses
Delivery Services	Organizations
Educational Consultants	Orientations
English Language Learners	Paraeducators
Entrepreneurs	Paralegals

Paramedics

Parent Teachers Associations

Pastors

Police Officers

Professional Development Trainers

Program Directors & Managers

Regional Managers

Sales Managers & Staff

School Leaders & Administrators

School Psychologists

School Principals

School Bus Drivers

School Teachers

Social Media Specialists

Small Businesses

Special Education Teams

Specialist Teachers

Sports Coaches

Students

Substitute Teachers

Supermarket Managers & Staff

Technology Specialists

Travel Agents

Truck Drivers

YouTubers

This book is dedicated to:

my parents: the late Joan & Leon Cannon, Sr.

my son: Ian the miracle baby

my siblings: Vet, Junie, Sandy & Mikki

book editors: Moneick and Keysha

professional contributors: Dana, Harvey and Rahmanda

friends, parents, teachers

athletic coaches, college adjuncts, colleagues

and the

organizations, schools, colleges and universities

who gave me an opportunity

to make a difference

in over 2,500+ students from Kindergarten to Kollege

"One's best success comes after their greatest disappointments."

Henry Ward Beecher

Preface

4/5/2018

My quest for helping students started when I was laid off from my job in 2000. I worked for the White House and was a program manager. Before then, I worked for a major bank in Philadelphia until 1998 and was laid off again.

Throughout my professional career, I'd been given a pink slip eight times up until now. What could I do to prevent further layoffs? My light bulb idea burned bright with solutions and ways to reinvent myself: I'll get into education and help students learn how to live in the 'real world.' And so the quest began!

But when I woke up to the perils of the broken education system, it dawned on me that I couldn't fix this. The government continued to put band-aids on *"No Child Left Behind,"* and state testing became teaching students how to pass the test and we slowly began to *fall behind* in the fool-proof designed academic curriculum.

As a first-year paraeducator, this was my first exposure to the education system. I was excited until I found out the pay was barely $14,000 per year! My last job paid $45,000 so I started in a deficit to survive and take care of my own little boy. I took on more part-time jobs so that I could have him with me at all times. Since I was a divorced mom, most jobs available were in education: after-school programs, tutoring help, chaperones on trips, and coaching sports.

As I travelled through the education's broken system, here's a reconstruction of what I found out through personal experiences over the last 18 years:

It's a very "Special Education"

Instructional specialists will sometimes "pull-out" the student and work on their education goals during the school day in small increments of time. Each child has an Individualized Education Plan (IEP) with academic goals to meet by the end of the school year. Reading, writing, social issues and learning/mental disabilities are revealed and monitored to help the student perform to the best of their ability in that grade level. Most students lag almost 2-3 grade levels behind so this task becomes more and more difficult as each year passes by. The end result: it starts all over again the next school year with a new date and new plan. Teachers are overwhelmed with so many students who need academic support and by state laws, they must be addressed with paper trails to show that they have at least reviewed the IEP with parents and offered resources to help the student improve areas that require the most remedial attention. In my assignment, I encountered many students who had fallen up to five grade levels behind. Most were bullies or students who looked like grown people with baby faces. When one big girl started to harass me, I was scared to go to work. She called me names, bumped into me on purpose and yelled constantly at me during class time. One day I overheard a student "rank" on another in the hallway and it worked. But how could I possibly stoop to her level to save my life and job? That night, I began 20 reasons to give her compliments. When she came in the next day, I put the class to work and she immediately called me skinny and ugly right off the bat. After that, I softly told her that I liked her dress. She was silent but her eyes quickly darted around the class. I softly told her that she would be pretty if she smiled more and frowned less. Then she nervously laughed. By the third compliment, she collapsed in my arms in tears. After that, we were best friends.

We all learned a lot in special education instruction that day and come to think of it, the dress was the ugliest I had ever seen yet I still had 17 more compliments to spare.......

Substitute Teaching

I was a substitute teacher for four years at various elementary, middle and high schools. The scary schools were quickly ousted from my list as I learned from the sub teachers who knew them best. It was $89 per day and $105 if I took a long-term sub position for a teacher out on leave. Most teachers did not leave plans so we had to improvise the best we could. If a class had disciplinary issues, the Dean of Students was notified only to *not* show up and we were left on our own perils. Most students saw us as an experiment to see if we would walk out since their regular teacher was absent so much. One student asked if I would stay because I actually gave the class a writing assignment and expected it to be finished by the end of class. Many teachers had not established student expectations or given guidelines to classroom management. That's when I started taking the long-term assignments. I finally felt like I was a part of something far greater in the education matrix. I established a teacher role and realized I liked it. By the time the original teacher returned, the students had adapted to my expectations and the teacher began to learn a lot from me plus action plans on what to do the following year.

Now, the teacher was in for the long haul and willing to genuinely commit to students, establish better communication with the parents, and give high fives for good behavior and improved academics in the classroom.......

Alternative Schools

A police officer is required to be in the classroom at all times for teacher safety. The mighty stench of homelessness, marijuana, cheap perfume and alcohol infiltrated my classroom like a dark plague. When a male student brushed up against me, called me a bitch and used abusive foul language I almost vomited in front of the whole class. He was only in the 8th grade! It was then that I knew that if it wasn't for my Bible left open on my desk and the daily scriptures I wrote on my chalkboard, I would have quit that long-term substitute position job months ago. My son was very young and my mortgage loomed every month so I had no choice but to stay. The student harassed me so much that I had to file a police report and he promised to punish me when I got to court for the misdemeanor hearing. My nerves were a wreck and my hair began to fall out due to the stress of the job and my inability to get employment elsewhere.

Most of the staff continued to hang on for retirement, others waited disability discharges and dedicated advisors were just worn out from the failing system.

I finished out my school year and read in the newspaper that the same student who harassed me later awaited a murder trial......

Christian Private Schools

I earned *"Outstanding Teacher of the Year"* at this cute little house on the prairie school. I was excited to get my first English teacher job in an *all-white* school. Everything was great until Dr. Martin Luther King Day rolled around and none of the students knew who he was so I gave an assignment to upper and lower grades. I thought it went well until Black History month emerged the first few days of February and I arranged for a trip to Baltimore for my classes to see a dramatic musical play in honor of the African-American culture. The students seemed to love it, at least that's what they told me until the bus discharged everyone at the front school entrance and a long line of parents snaked along the hallway to the principal's office. When I went to see what the commotion was about, I saw angry faces and fists shaking in the air at the principal over the cultural exposure. Later, the principal somehow changed her mind about the "good idea" field trip we both agreed to. I was good at teaching and tutoring the students who couldn't read or write. I loved them like they were my very own children. Our yearbook represented diversity in the school and my "teacher presence" held true. I was discreetly voted to earn this award and stood firm on my faith that God sent me to teach a needed lesson about *equality* regardless of skin color. In my heart, they needed to learn and know about a great man such as Dr. Martin Luther King, Jr. and that if they expected to graduate high school, they had to know how to read and write—as a result, the school won an essay contest for the first time. I'll never forget the hugs I received on my last day of school. I'll never forget the tears on a mother's face when she rushed back to the cafeteria so that no one would see her hugging and thanking me for discreetly tutoring her son. How could such a *cute* little school on the prairie filled with loving staff who smiled and welcomed me on the first day of school be stuck in the 1930's with the same *ugly* prejudices my parents endured?

I guess that's just how the wind blows over there on the prairie so the following school year a new black principal just happened to fairy dust his way in .....

Charter Schools

There's something about having millions of dollars in a school budget that triggers excitement in school administrators. For some, $10,000 per student is the gateway to building a great academic empire to ensure education for all to succeed in the "real-world." For others, it lines their purses with revenue that isn't theirs to keep. Some charters get to pick the student population: all black, all white, mixed and other. It's hard to believe that there are widely respected administrators who steal, change grades, manipulate others, and dominate the educational matrix. I feel for the parents who are left still trying to figure out the mystery of another charter school that is taken over by the Department of Education to realign and redesign the school's official mission and reach a lost community yet to start all over again. Some administrators are sent to jail and publicly reprimanded for inappropriate financial spending behaviors. Staff grieve their job loss and comfort parents in disbelief while law suits continue to mound. It eventually begins to fall apart and tumbles down like

Jericho's walls. I often wondered what happened to their passion in the beginning to build a great school and then lose it to educational corruption. It just ends up hurting everyone, especially the sacred family structure and foundation in which it is was first built.

What an oxymoron for the <u>*ignorant educator*</u> *and the corrupted definition of why today's families truly need strong academic foundations for a good education…..*

Schools for Girls

Whether you wear a private school uniform or a frilly pink maternity dress, most girls either go to school giggling or using foul language like sailors together. Since there are no boys around, learning should take place. And it does, when they are ready to learn. As a teacher, I learned that middle school and high school girls are feisty and very street smart for their young age. Some students have to change social behaviors if they desire an education and steady career to take care of an unborn child. Some have two children and some have had abortions. My experience with this population caused me much stress since they also bullied me and other teachers. They used profanity, smoked marijuana, manipulated the school system, banned together in times exams, tests and quizzes, and fought failing grades due to non-participation in the classroom. Even though it was an *all-girls* school, I often wondered how they found those boys.

Someone's little girl made it to the university driving a Mercedes Benz carrying a pink designer handbag instead of a baby's car seat in tow………

School Districts

In. Out. In. Out. When you travel through revolving doors, it's just that simple. It continues to "revolve" and does not "resolve" anything but a continued vicious cycle of disorganization. I didn't understand district dynamics until I experienced day-to-day activities of the staff and teachers who were regularly paid. However, after three months of working, I did not get paid one shiny red cent. My mortgage fell behind, my car was almost repossessed and my home phone nearly disconnected. In tears, I bravely walked into my boss' office, sat down and blew my snotty nose until it turned red. He was just too busy to wrap this up when I first came on board. After several hours of sitting, crying and nervously rocking myself back to sanity, I realized that this was not acceptable. The secretary came in rubbing my back to soothe away all the ugly inconvenience and accepted full responsibility for being irresponsible. I walked away with a freshly cut check and off I went to repair the damage to my stellar credit rating of 802 which plummeted to a mere 658. Just as I was finally put on the district payroll system, I received a pink slip announcing that my services were no longer needed due to cut backs in leadership transitions at the end of the school year.

Not because of my job performance, but financial mistrust of school funds and unmet academic goals were left in a chaotic pile.......

Athletics and Coaching

I played basketball. Even racked up a few kudos: First Team All-Conference, Most Valuable Player, Most in Media, First Team All-State, Blue/Gold Team and helped win a girls basketball division conference title. We managed to make it to the First-Round Quarter Finals but lost from sheer fright. Shortly after, I was invited to practice with a university women's team and my coach went with me to see how I would fare against collegiate talent. As scared as I was to step in that huge stadium, the university coach greeted me with a big grin. An hour later, I proudly left with 15 points and 10 rebounds all in my beat up old gym bag. True talent doesn't go away, it just gets better when it becomes unleashed. Years later, I played basketball at a YMCA although men didn't welcome women on the teams very often. You had to prove yourself first. *Shirts or Skins?* Of course shirts, I was a lady for goodness sakes! In the corporate world I played in a professional sports arena to raise money. I later got into basketball coaching and was a JV Boys Basketball Head Coach, High School Varsity Girls Basketball Head Coach, Assistant Women's Basketball Coach at a community college and volunteer coach for girls AAU Basketball teams. I knew what it was like for athletes to combine academics in order to make a holistic athlete. Grades were like Gatorade: it quenched the thirst for knowledge and kept their butts on the team! As a coach, I could monitor their progress, see the teacher, and discipline through practice. I could see them November through February and know exactly who was failing and who skipped class. After the season was over, so was the coach/athlete relationship and then it would start all over in the fall. *Athletes need support and academic resources to keep the learning going.* Just like the game, if you don't practice your foul shots, it could cost the game in the final minutes. In school, it works the same. Reading and writing must be practiced daily or it gets lost. *If players sit the bench, coaches can't win championships or make it to Sweet 16's or Final Four appearances.* As an educator, I also know that if athletes can't read or write, their lives will be a continuous financial struggle unless they get educational support and the basic resources they need.

Should college athletes get paid?" Maybe they should since some coaches get paid bonuses from teams taking them to Final Four Championships free of charge……

Real Reason Good Teachers, Instructors and Adjuncts Leave Education

When I was growing up in the 70's, most parents and the community expected a few things out of their children. First, they were to get a high school education, a job, and start a family—in that order. In other words, you were expected to get out of the house <u>because it was your turn.</u> If you didn't get a job, then you could opt to stay at home and further your education. After that, you could move out and do your own thing. You could *only* stay home if you were disabled, mentally ill or had to care for a family member. If you were pregnant prior to being married, you were sent away and came back slim and trim again. Expectations didn't change; you still had to have a future plan.

Today, most educators stay in the field for 20-40 years because they love teaching and seeing their students prosper in the real world. Most retire but stay in some form of educational pursuit to keep their minds sharp and abreast of future trends. Unfortunately they have not been able to see what currently lies in the desks and chairs of our new age students. Today's educators have the expectation of developing and creating quality work at the high school and college levels. They want the 6+1 Writing Traits memorized and defined in essays and research papers. The mechanics and usage are clearly understood: a well-developed thesis, an abstract page, and credible sources for the reference page which should total 15-20 pages with a cover sheet.

In reality, today's teachers are lucky to even get the paper on time without an anxiety of backlash for being too strict on deadlines, assignment expectations, and providing specific guideline rubrics. Too many assignments bring on too many complaints while class participation enhances lost social skills needed to perform in the workforce. There's no time to complete a final project because students are "busy" and let alone even bother to come to class. *As a result, good teachers, instructors, and adjuncts leave the profession they love because the school system has failed to teach the basics of reading, writing and 'rithmetic leaving the classroom teacher in a bind to combat behavior issues, teach the curriculum and prepare for state tests.*

I had the opportunity to talk with former educators who left the classroom from elementary to college. Here's a reconstructed response of what they genuinely shared (names have been protected for their privacy):

University Professor/English

"For years I kept asking for quality college work and effort but students came in with the basic high school mentality of just getting by. Most weren't ready for college. Even though my passion was teaching, it was time to change gears doing something else at the university level."

Retired Principal/Middle School

"The system failed a long time ago, especially in the inner city schools. We just couldn't keep up with the school climate and suspensions. We had a long list of issues so we did the best we could with the resources we had. We ended up losing a lot of good teachers in the process."

Special Education Teacher/High School

"My class size was too big and it was hard to monitor every IEP learning goal. Some were homeless and suffering abuse from parents, relatives or caregivers. Clothes, food and safety became more important than learning in the classroom. The kids in my room needed love and attention more than anything else. After bringing concerns home every night to my own family, that's when I knew it was time to find another profession."

English Adjunct/Community College

"English papers were always below the college reading level. Students are put in remedial classes but only so much can be done when a skill has not been learned like basic sentences, punctuation and capitalization. Students write the way they text and talk and college may not be the right fit. I feel like I'm back teaching middle school again. It's just no longer a true college experience anymore."

Art Teacher/Charter School

"I tried to hang in there because I dreamed of teaching students the many facets of art culture and fun projects to find artistic careers. Instead, they tore up my room, destroyed my supplies and laughed at me when I tried to discipline. At least I lasted 3 months…some of my peers could barely make it to three weeks."

Online Courses

You can always tell a student's work ethic. After teaching online courses, most students failed simply because they refused to make the commitment. The ones who passed were on grade level and missed class either for an illness or emergency. When I followed up, they were glad to hear from me and came in to get 1-on-1 instruction when they needed it. On the other hand, the non- passing students wanted to know why I was following up and told me to back off. Some parents like to help with the lesson unit and tests. How did I know? When I ask specific questions about the lesson, the student had no clue. When I asked the parent, the lesson was well versed and easily summarized. Most online programs always show the amount of time spent on the lessons, the grade received for tests, and unit-by-unit completion. As a teacher, it bothered me that some parents put it into their own hands to get a child graduated. If not, it would be another repeated failure of Grade 12. Guess I still believe that if students complete the course, he/she could feel the satisfaction that hard work really does pay off and they could accomplish so much more by mere effort. As graduation came to a close, the student sheepishly walked over to me trying not to cry. They finally took the online wheel and finished the course without parental assistance and wanted to make things right. A lesson was learned which bore genuine integrity, character and hard work required to make it in the real world. I beamed like an old mother hen and hugged her shoulders tight as tears streamed down her pretty little face. Her parents looked confused but I simply waved away the concern with a big teacher smile.

As I walked away from that little girl trying to become a responsible young woman, I realized then why I became an educator in the first place and cried all the way home........

English as a Second Language (ESL)**

I took the attendance and couldn't pronounce one first name. The last names were easy. Maybe I bit off more than I could chew at the university level. Many things began to bother me about my new class and the daunting tasks that came with it. First, the pre-tests and quizzes all had many spelling and grammatical errors and the syllabus had not been updated in a while. Much of the material had been cut and pasted, page numbers confused, and themes outdated. When I challenged my class, I got e-mails to *Please See Me* from my advisor. When I asked them to put away their cell phones in class, I was summoned to *Please See Me* again. When we talked about student expectations, I assured administration that my ethics were not going to be changed, classroom management would be maintained, and that learning would take place whether my students were in attendance or not. I stood by my integrity as an instructor.

One student was a former teacher but grammar and spelling had not caught up with her credentials from Argentina. Every grade was challenged and debated, homework assignments scrutinized, and creative, yet newfound ways to get more points came across my desk every week. When I finally got over intimidation tactics and eye rolling, she slowly melted into fine-tuned mutual respect and backed off. I supplemented my lessons, played word games, and collaborated on assignments. Most of all, I taught them study skills and brought writing resources to use outside of class. I took them to university events to practice introducing themselves and challenged them to try outside activities and share with the class. I helped them with time management since some had children and worked up to three part-time jobs. By the end of the semester, they said I was a great teacher. Even Ms. Argentina*.

They learned my name that semester. I was no longer Ms. Teacher. I was Ms. Scott, ESL extraordinaire…..

**I have also taught and tutored ESL students from the following countries: Africa, Brazil, China, Columbia, England, France, Germany, India, Japan, Mexico, Morocco, Peru, Puerto Rico, Saudi Arabia and Spain.

Online K-12 Schools

Every time an online school commercial comes on the television, I automatically sit up and look at the "paid actors" who make such learning fun. The principal reassures parents that their child's education is top notch and his education team will be available 24-hours/7 days a week just for your family. That's what parent/teacher conferences were for along with the quarterly report card Christmas present that either carried "coal" or "candy" in the report card packet: <u>Your child is passing or failing. See Teacher Comments.</u> The part in the commercial that really bothered me the most was how passionate the students were about being able to actually *stay at home and spend more time with their families.* I guess I thought a child should be in school interacting with other children to learn diversity, culture and social skills to develop for the real-world. They should be working with other children to learn how to share, observe, respect authority and learn new information together. These same children grow up together, ride the bus together, explore fun field trips together, graduate together, and later have their own families and then the education cycle starts all over again. On the other hand, some online schools can foster student isolation and give complete permission for "parent teachers" which is very similar to homeschooling. In some cases, homeschooling can have a dynamic lesson structure coupled with exciting activities, sports and extracurricular options. Some parents even hold Education degrees and have classroom experience to understand the dynamics and work that goes into teaching a year-long core curriculum. If this is the new "wave" of the educational future, perhaps parents are simply fed up with the public school system which is still leaving "many children behind" and can forge ahead to a new school frontier experience in cyberspace. If parents think the latest iPhone is a distraction to get their kids to sit down together at the dinner table, just wait until it's time to set the rules to do the *online* homework while encouraging their child to "put the phone away" using their **outdoor** voice like the teachers do in the real-world elementary, middle and high school classroom.

I'm willing to bet that parents will quickly enroll their child back into the public school after being home with them after a few months and really appreciate waiting at the bus stop in the morning in any kind of weather…...

Tutor, Tutor Stay on Your Pencil-Shaped Scooter

Parents say that they will pay anything for a good tutor. I started out $10 an hour and barely got my money after the session was over. When I earned my Master's degree, I went to $25 and was nervous about saying the amount for fear they would turn me down. At my last networking seminar, my mentor ripped into me like the wind. Why wasn't I charging $50-$89 an hour as a Learning Coach? After lunch and wiping away my sorry tears, I walked out with more confidence than ever before. I knew that I brought *value*, *specialized skills* and *experience* that no other tutor could match. I have repeat clients who know my credibility, integrity and expertise. I offer a holistic approach to academics and *The Learning Coach* is my small business mantra. If parents or students want a $15 tutor, there are plenty of those yellow *tutor scooters* available for cheap. But if they desire a certified academic writing coach who interacts with the child's teacher, attends teacher/parent conferences, collaborates with the high school Guidance Departments, offers academic counseling, finds scholarships, teaches college essay strategies from *Kindergarten to Kollege* in each session to use the strategies in the classroom to succeed, *then those are the clients who are welcome to inquire.* Quality. Value. Guaranteed return on your investment since 2005.

Why this guidebook was written

When I ask parents what their child's education is worth, I usually get a satisfying response until we start getting down to the real reason the child is behind in the first place. Parents have known their children's capabilities since birth in comparison to their other children. When this is revealed, it is crucial to get help at the onset of an educational imbalance.

For example, if a child cannot recognize all 26 letters of the alphabet in **pre- school by the age of four** or identify upper case or lower case letters, parents are provided detailed strategies on how to practice these important skills at home early in the education process. As children move to the next level, the **kindergarten** teacher will test the student to see if they can recognize upper and lower case letters and write their name using capital and lower case letters legibly. The funny thing is that the teacher continues to tell parents educational short falls and many times offers suggestions, supplements, tutors, etc. to help the child become **first grade** ready. The next question is what will the parent do? Answer: Either *fight* (get help right away) or *flight* (deal with it later).

Here's the problem: parents *already know* if their child falls into one of these categories:

- Poor alphabet recognition (upper and lower case letters)

- Unable to write name legibly

- Unable to comprehend main ideas in stories or books

- Unable to recognize basic sight words (I, me, see, at, etc.)

- Behavioral issues in classroom

- Failing grades

- Held back from next grade promotion or failed previous grade

- Learning disabilities with Individualized Education Plan (IEP)

Early identification and mastery at the third grade level is **proof that a child has or has not developed these skills to successfully graduate high school** and might not be able to perform at the college level. It is not a secret. Ask any parent and you will get the same response: "He's always been a sloppy writer." "She has never liked to read." Parents have always known.

That's why this guidebook is so important to parents and educators and anyone who has to write in their career, profession, academics and anything else that requires written communication skills basics from middle school, high school or **first-year college**.

The whole point of this book is designed with a willingness to start over regardless of what you learned or didn't learn in school. Some students didn't learn by circumstance. Some just need a brush-up and review. Some even hate to write and need something to guide their own children or others to be college ready. <u>Whatever it was for you, here it is now.</u>

Since 2005, I have provided academic support to over 2,500 students and athletes. Some think of me as a "glorified tutor" who blings. I offer parents, working adults, students, athletes and professionals a guide to be better writers and business communicators. I have authored two (working on my third) books, was acknowledged by President Obama for handwriting achievements, nominated *Outstanding Teacher of the Year* and shook hands with Delaware Governor John Carney in his 2019-20 educational initiative for all children to succeed.

If you are still reading this, I commend you. Now you can understand why I must continue my quest in offering a resource to our schools, colleges and universities the real meaning of why all parents want their children to have a "good education." That was also my parents' reason for seeing that we got one, too. Now, I'm seeing to it that you and others receive the same.

So, turn the page to the table of contents and start with your own reasons "From Kindergarten to Kollege in 10 Steps!"

All My Educational Best,

Pamelyn Smythscott, M.Ed.

Pamelyn Smythscott, M.Ed.

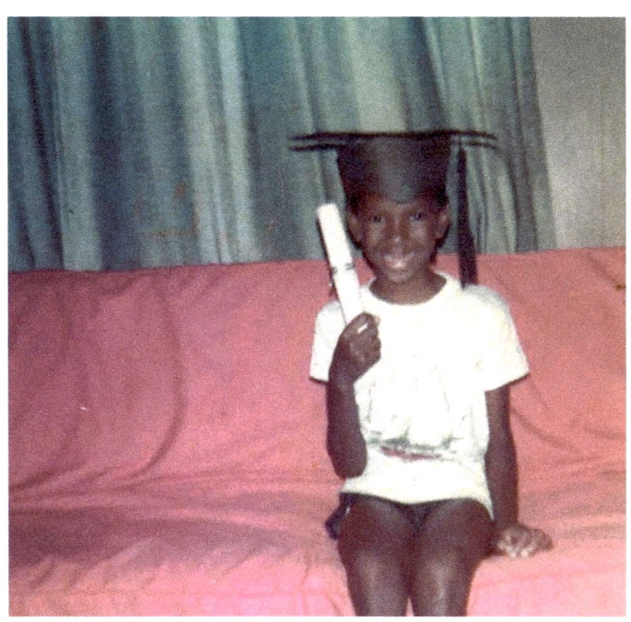

Introduction

Just when we thought the Technology Age could fix everything, someone still must write a proposal, sign for the new equipment or outline an agenda for a virtual, in-person staff meeting, impromptu or formal gathering.

Still don't believe it?

Let's take a look at our modern day world and how writing (whether you hen-peck it in on the computer or physically write it in) is required at home, business, work and school:

- Write a letter—return address, envelope address and cursive signature
- Thank you note—few sentences
- Text Message—slang responses and abbreviations (lol)
- Certified mail—complete postal info and cursive signature
- Diaries—secret thoughts written
- Ledgers—business documents noted
- Legal documents—cursive signature
- Magazine subscription—complete form and return
- Prescriptions (Rx)—cursive signature for medication
- Grocery list—even on a phone, you have to spell
- Driver's License—cursive signature
- Passport—application and cursive signature
- UPS package—signature (now they just leave it)
- Notes, Memos & Stickies—handwritten reminders
- Business Cards—cleverly written to promote business
- Flyers & Newsletters—written promotions
- Junk Mail—cleverly written graphics to clutter your house
- New job—application, forms completed and cursive signature
- Workshops, courses or classes—taking notes

- Oral presentation—write speech/fill out evaluation/write comments
- Registration—sign-in, complete forms and cursive signature
- Library card—complete application and cursive signature
- Lottery or Prizes—complete forms and cursive signature
- New car—complete documents, forms and cursive signed agreements
- E-mails—written response required
- E-mail address—complete registration for new account
- New Cell Phone—application and signature
- Weddings—send back RSVP envelope handwritten
- Doctor, Hospital, & Surgical forms—requires legible printing
- Funerals—complete insurance forms and cursive signature
- Auto Insurance—complete application and cursive signature
- Websites, blogs—requires writing in sentences/paragraphs
- Power Points—requires phrases, titles and examples
- Returns and Refunds—requires signature and completed form
- Speeding Ticket—requires cursive signature
- Personal, Employer or Business Check—requires cursive signature to cash
- Money Order—requires completing form and cursive signature
- Laboratory Blood Work—complete forms and cursive signature
- Personal Check—fill in date, amount (written amount must match numerical amount), memo and cursive signature
- Rental Car—requires cursive signature and application
- Hotel Reservation—requires cursive signature and registration form
- Car Repairs—requires cursive signature
- Marriage or Death Certificate—cursive signatures
- Contracts & Agreements—cursive signature
- Medical Emergency Forms—cursive signature
- Justice of the Peace or Court Appearances—forms and cursive signature
- Online ordering—complete forms
- Restaurant bill—cursive signature on check
- Conference Name Tag—printed signature
- Publishing a book—writing and more writing!

I'm sure the list can go on and on. But isn't this a fine start? I believe that writing will always play a major part of our communication skills and stabilize its worth throughout the educational process just like mathematics, science, and technology. From pre-school we are taught the 26 letters of the *alphabet* and their sounds then go on to *sight words* to make words and build sentences. Through those basic reading and writing strategies our vocabulary increases to read and write more fluently to compete in our global world of communication and social media.

So as we travel through the complexities of today's American educational system, this book will take you "From Kindergarten to Kollege" in 10 basic steps to help you understand each grade level and the requirements for promotion. So, turn the page so that we can get started. You'll also note that there's no signature required, at least not until Chapter one!

Contents

CHAPTER 1

Step 1: Learn basic writing (cursive and print/manuscript) skills to complete school assignments, employment applications, office work,forms, applications and legal documents as required by law.

Chapter 1

Poor Writing in America: Legible Writing Starts in Third Grade

Can you put your John Hancock here, please?

Cursive handwriting is slowly coming back into public schools. Since it was taken out, most students still do not know how to read in cursive or cannot legibly write their signature *(known as their John Hancock)* which is often required on important legal documents.

You are scheduled to attend a workshop or networking activity and the first person at the door says, "Please sign in!" Most of the signatures look like chicken scratch so you add yours to the list. In this chapter, you will review the basics of legible handwriting in case you have not practiced in a while. Here is the first lesson in 7 S's of Handwriting as a refresher:

The 7 S's of Handwriting

1. Signature   *Signature*

This is your John Hancock in cursive format (letters joined together) needed for important legal documents

2. Size   SIZE

These are **tall** letters in the alphabet (b,d,f,h,k,l,t) and the rest are **short**. They should be distinguished in writing, not all the same size on paper

3. Shape   **Shape**

This is how you make letters. Are they neat and consistent or uneven and confusing?

4. Slant   *Slant*

This is how you hold your paper; if right handed, turn paper to the left. If left handed, turn paper to the right to get the slanted look on paper

5. Space   *Space*

This is the spacing between letters and words; they shouldn't be smashed together but open and neat for legibility

6. Speed   *Speed*

This is how fast you write while staying legible

7. Sloppy   *Sloppy*

This is handwriting that is hard to read or follow in cursive or print

Next, you will review the 26 letters of the alphabet in manuscript style or print. If you still don't believe that this is really the alphabet, visit a grade classroom and check our the paper they use with the red dotted lines to understand their tall (b, d, f, h, k, l, and t) letters and how to properly write their names using capital and lower case letters. I've written them for you since most people don't pay attention to the basics which leads to handwriting that is not legible:

Handwritten by *The Learning Coach, LLC 2019*

Handwritten by *The Learning Coach, LLC 2019*

Camel Humps

m, n, v, x, u

Ocean Waves

a, c, d, g

Roller Coasters

b, f, h, j, k, l

Mountain Tops

i, t, r, w

Curls & Twirls

o, q, e

Cursive Graphic Organizer

Created by *The Learning Coach, LLC 2018*

Research shows that teachers and professors give better grades to papers they can read! These same students also have better scores on their Math SAT test. Handwriting is a "cognitive skill" which is why I still teach handwriting in tutoring to refresh high school and college students on the basics. As early as pre-school, students learn how to hold a pencil correctly. If they hold it in an awkward way, their handwriting becomes difficult to read and it's hard to reverse this technique by third or fourth grades.

Unfortunately, poor handwriting continues to plague our country and has become the norm. Since this is a "cognitive skill," most students do not get to experience cursive writing in elementary school because technology is infiltrating the classroom as a whole. However, handwriting is still a complex skill to learn and it is a very simple motor skill that must be used daily which helps with reading, writing and spelling—all very important core subjects in elementary school.

In Great Britain, cursive is required and most private schools across America still teach it throughout high school. *Psychology Today.com* supports children's literacy and academic development because it improved spelling and written composition. Another important skill is that writing helps with memorization, especially after a teacher models a student's first and last name with proper capitalization and spelling. It is then that the student begins to remember it by heart. Now that's teaching at its best!

However, today's younger generation cannot read in cursive. I've tried to write my name on the whiteboard at the college level and hands quickly go up to ask the burning question, "*What is that on the board?*" Others soon look at me wide-eyed waiting for an answer and then I write the same letters in manuscript (or print) beneath my cursive to help them understand:

Welcome to English 101   *Ms. Smythscott*

Welcome to English 101   Ms. Smythscott

Read Unit 3, Page 104

Read Unit 3, Page 104

Complete Questions 1-5

Complete Questions 1-5

When finished, select your end of semester project

When finished, select your end of semester project

Criminal Cursive

When I taught handwriting, I came across a reconstructed article that read:

"Bank Stunned by Robber's Handwritten Note"

I made a copy and taped it to my whiteboard for open discussion with my students. The bank robber's handwriting was so bad that the bank teller asked him to rewrite the note at least two times. In frustration, he tried to write it again, but by the time he got the note together and gave it back to the bank teller, he was in handcuffs and dragged to jail.

Grade 3—Reconstructed Constitution assignment, this student wrote
an opinion about laws and how to handle President Donald Trump

If I Could Write the

Constitution

I would write my own law or rule and say.....

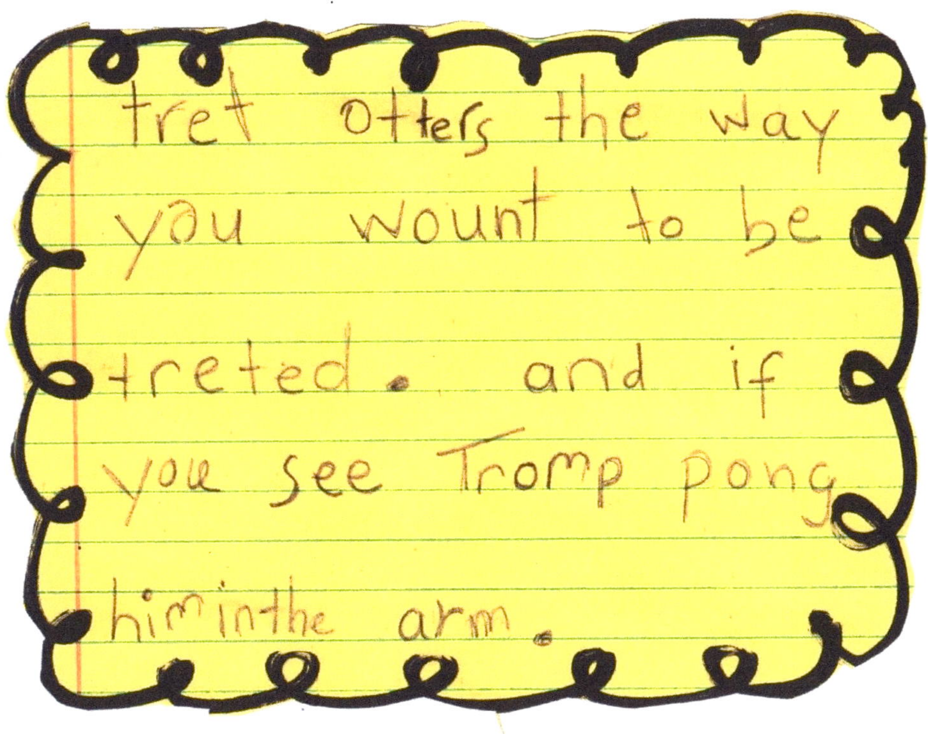

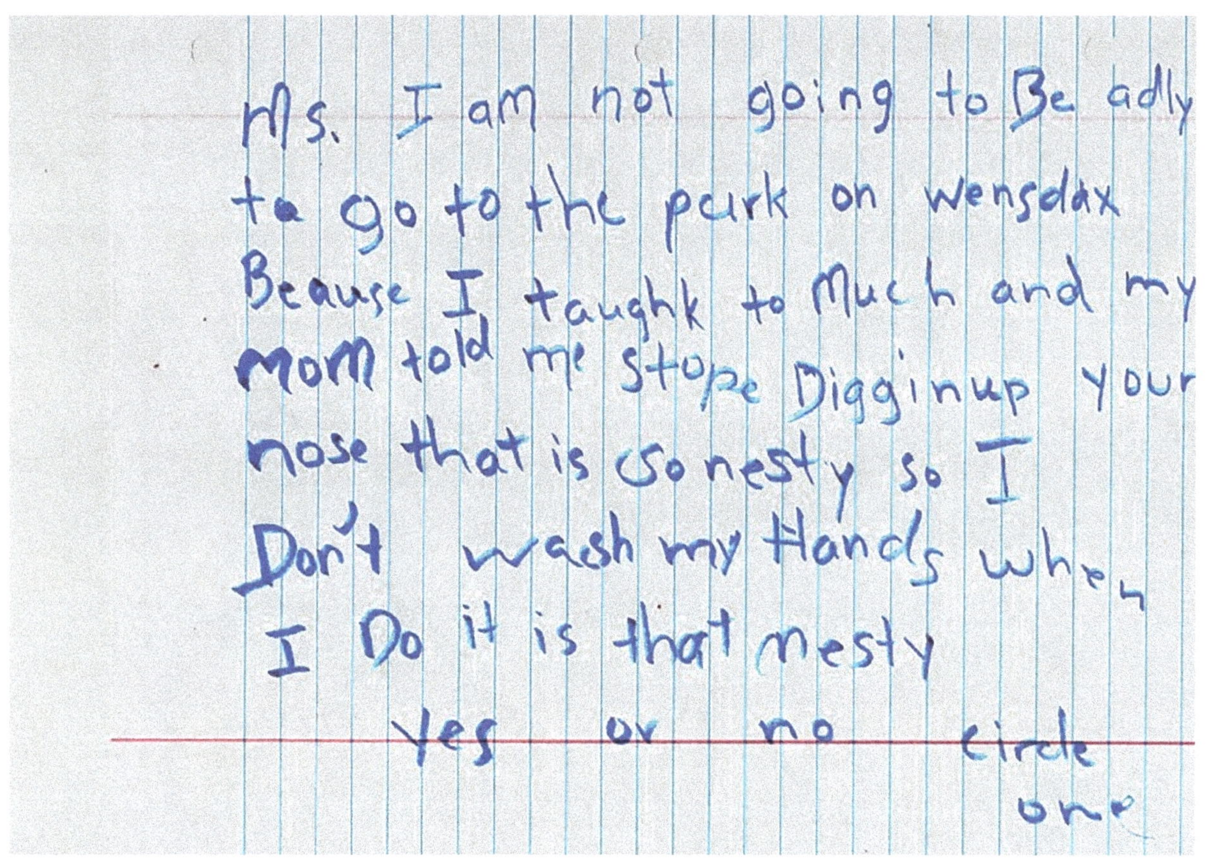

Grade 4—Reconstructed student note to elementary teacher
explaining reasons for not going on the field trip

Grade 9—Reconstructed student response to a writing
assignment for a 5 paragraph essay

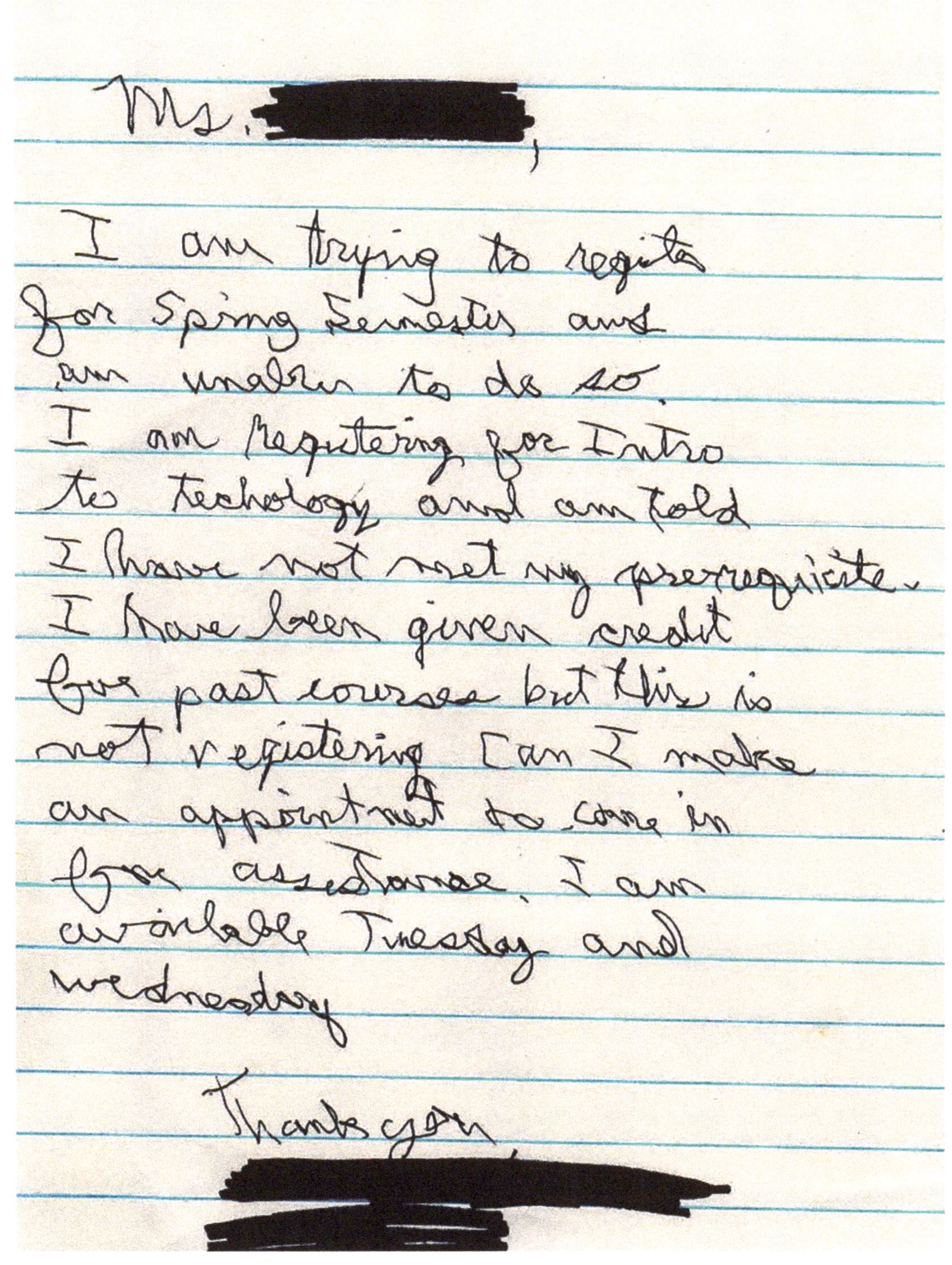

Ms. ████████,

I am trying to register
for Spring Semester and
am unable to do so.
I am registering for Intro
to Technology and am told
I have not met my prerequisite.
I have been given credit
for past courses but this is
not registering Can I make
an appointment to come in
for assistance. I am
available Tuesday and
Wednesday

Thank you,
████████

University—Reconstructed student email to the professor
explaining why the last assignment was late

> Good day Ma,
>
> My weekend was great, I as sorry assignment is a later date.
> Above is where my student work is.
>
> Thanks, Pa

Just when you thought writing <u>wasn't important</u>, it happens in our everyday lives! Here are some more examples of using our signature or using some form of the writing process:

- Broken leg—sign on the cast
- Birthday cards—sign with a phrase
- Chalk or White board—requires legible writing
- Field trip permission slip—requires signature
- Newspaper subscription—requires signature
- Furniture delivery—requires signature
- Name on child's lunch box or in clothes
- Business mailing labels
- Labeling a file folder tab
- Labeling a bin or organizer
- Writing in a day planner or organizer daytimer
- Signing your Social Security Card
- Signing your debit card on the back
- Flu Shot—fill out form and signature
- Doctor's office—sign in
- Starting new job—fill out paperwork, W-2's, and lab work
- Secret Santa—write your name and gift request
- Book signing—John Hancock, please!

So the next time you are in the grocery store and the cashier asks for your "John Hancock" to sign your debit card, your signature will always remain an important part of your identity for merchants, government or legal documents, postal services, and more.

Did you Know that.....

....many millennials cannot write or even read in cursive since it has been taken out of most public schools by third grade?

....handwriting analysis is the "key' to criminal investigations, financial frauds and white collar crimes?

....learning how to write in cursive improves academic success?

....teachers, professors and instructors give better grades to handwritten worksheets/papers they can read?

....some students have better scores on math and SAT (cognitive development)?

....handwriting wasn't taught until around the mid-19th century which was when free public school started?

....printing in schools didn't start until around the 1940's and cursive originated from Italic calligraphy handwriting?

....all business & government correspondence was once done in spectacular penmanship and considered a valued job skill?

....Coca-Cola and Ford still use the Spencerian Script in their logos today?

WORD of the Day: GRAPHOLOGY—a study of handwriting looked upon as an expression of a writer's character, personality and abilities; examining handwriting can also tell what kind of person you are

Your Turn Activity:

1. **Write a handwritten personal letter** to an older relative in your best print or cursive handwriting. (Do you know the 5 parts of a letter?)

Date   **Salutation**   **Body**   **Closing**   **Signature**

____

____

____

____

____

____

____

2. **In your next meeting or class, have everyone "sign-in"** and see how many names were written legibly. (See if they print, write in cursive, or chicken scratch)

Sign-In Sheet

Name	Department/Course
1.	
2.	

3. **Retrieve an application form** (library card, college registrar, employment) and do your best to **complete the required information** in the small spaces (Remember the 6 S's of handwriting for legibility)

Chapter 1 Notes

Step 2: Read daily (starting at the age of two) and be read to (with expression, fluency and comprehension are key).

Chapter 2

Old Skool Still Works: Dick, Jane & Spot Had a Good Life

What happens when a child can't read by third grade?

They see "Jane and Spot run" and then "mother and father run with Spot" to the nearest library for beginner reader books.

If a child can't read fluently by the end of grade three, parents should consult a tutor and enroll in an academic camp to keep up the learning process while it is still early. If not, the child will continue to read below grade level and worsen by the time they reach middle school.

Many parents know that their child cannot read in the first grade but often fail to do anything about it until it is too late. Students can easily pick up on slow learners in the class who are not confident to read in front of others or in a group. When this happens, the teacher will reach out to the parents in a conference to discuss the seriousness of getting academic support before it is too late. I have experienced this many times during teacher/parent conferences and my suggestions for getting a tutor go unheard. Here are the **top three reconstructed excuses**:

"Look, I've got other children to take care of. They'll grow out of it like I did."

"Tutors are expensive. He can learn more by playing sports than learning school books."

"If I spend my hard earned money on a tutor, I expect fast results. Can you guarantee that this will work even though my child is way behind?"

Here are some more …..

"My child's always been slow to catch on. Tutoring is a waste of time. Let's just wait until middle school."

"It doesn't matter about poor handwriting as long as the teacher can read it."

"There's no difference between a tutor and a learning coach. I just want the cheapest rate per hour."

Hang on for the high school level….

"We'll worry about getting help next year when he/she gets to college."

"Let the coach worry about the grades. He's worked hard to get this sports scholarship."

"What's wrong with a 2.0 G.P.A.? She'll get better in college."

"The IEP wasn't monitored in middle school. I hope it will be better now."

Dick, Jane and Spot Had a Good Life

Of course Spot can't talk but you better believe that he knew that Jane was an excellent reader! Her brother Dick was even better because their parents insisted on reading when they first began to talk. Between *Dick and Jane Stories* in the 1930's, *Weekly Readers* and *The Cat in the Hat* in the 1950's, millions of preschoolers and kindergarteners (like me and my sisters) read those books sitting on my dad's lap over and over again. Their sole purpose was to expose young students to basic vocabulary, phonetics, vowel sounds and sight words. To help with reading, the characters were very colorful and their adventures were small problems that ended with a happy solution through gentle guidance from mother and father. Basic comprehension of these simple stories helped make reading fun. The *Dick, Jane and Spot* collection titles always started with a verb: <u>See</u> Jane Run, <u>See</u> Spot Go, or *See* Sally Play. In *The Cat in the Hat*, rhyming sounds were important to learning new words and repeating sounds throughout the story. Spelling was easier since it became a sight word combined with blended sounds for a silly story. When put together, these basic **leveled readers** enabled any child to develop self-confidence which made reading exciting and fun.

In elementary school, we couldn't wait to get our *Weekly Readers* from *Scholastic* which was our miniature version of the newspaper and basic source of the latest news in the classroom. It was first published in September 21, 1928 and introduced in classrooms throughout the 1930's into the 1960's.

But before the basic readers, most American families owned and read the one and only common book, the Bible which was printed in its original form and hard to read since it was set in Old English and translated from Latin. For children, the *Weekly Reader* became our "Bible" for learning about new inventions, travels to space, animal species and supplemented our Social Studies curriculum with fun activities, projects and lessons to share with our families. Its colorful pictures and new vocabulary proved fascinating which helped young readers grow into chapter books, explore science careers, dream of futuristic technology and make learning fun.

Our curiosity expanded into more complex reading which led to the Britannica Encyclopedia collection ranging from various subjects and topics in hardback textbooks from A-Z. Like today's internet, this was also our biggest and most up to date resource used for research and educational purposes in the classroom.

Understanding Phonics, Phonetics and Vowels

The *basic vowel sounds* in our English language are **a, e, i, o and u**. These sounds can also be *long* or *short*. Here's an example:

Long a sound	ate		Short a sound	bat
Long e sound	eat		Short e sound	bed
Lone i sound	ice		Short i sound	it
Long o sound	soon		Short o sound	son
Long u sound	blue		Short u sound	but

How we Learn:
Visual, Audio and Kinesthetic

When we were growing up, the Old Skool methods worked! But today, more and more students fall behind in reading because they cannot always practice classroom strategies at home since parents are working longer hours and children are in daycare or after-school programs. Homework was and still is a very important component to learning key concepts in the academic curriculum. However, some parents may argue that schools give "too much" homework which is impossible to complete after school. So, if parents are getting home after 5 p.m., it is hard for them to pick up the kids, get dinner started, begin homework or start a project, get ready for the next day *and* put everyone to bed by 9 p.m. No wonder parents collapse on the couch! They still haven't had a chance to open the mail, check phone messages, clean up the kitchen, pick up in cluttered rooms or spend time with their significant other. I remember coming home from school and changing out of my "good school clothes," doing my assigned chores and starting my homework at the dinner table. My mother was making dinner and my siblings were somewhere in the house doing their homework, too. After dinner and homework was done, we could go outside and play until dusk. But if homework wasn't done, the dinner table was where you stayed until the homework was checked by my mom. Since I struggled with math, we did 3-digit addition and subtraction until I had cramped hands and dreamt about numbers in my sleep! I read the *Dick and Jane* books until my dad couldn't take it anymore and gently pushed me off his lap to enjoy his pipe and settle in to watch *Gunsmoke* promptly at 8 p.m.

Here's a look at *Old Skool* vs. *New Skool* regarding academics, behavior and pedogogy (teaching):

Old Skool Pedogogy	New Skool Pedogogy
Teacher said, "Put on your thinking caps" for creativity and imagination	Now teacher says, "This helps you with critical thinking skills"
After reading a book, students wrote a book report to understand main idea	After reading a book or story, students go back to find the support or evidence
Cursive writing was taught and practiced in Grade 3	Most students in Grades 3-12 cannot write or read in cursive
School plays and holiday speeches developed expressive public speaking and communication skills	Power Points, video conferencing and Facetime are the new presentations
Go outside! Activities and games like cowboys & Indians, tag, hide & seek, hop scotch, double-dutch & hand clapping songs (Mary Mack) inspired creativity, imagination and hand/eye coordination	Stay inside! Play videos, binge watch T.V. shows for hours, stay on your phone, send text messages, pick up/ look at iPhone 125 times a day
Readers' Theatre: auditioned with dramatic expression/wore costume before a live classroom	Reading is not the most favorite; many read monotone on long passages, short stories, and chapter books
If handwriting was not legible, work was not accepted; student would have to rewrite	If handwriting is not legible, students must type on a Word document
Students didn't visit the principal's office; it was only pointed out passing by in the hallway during school tours	Principals are online with offices in cyberspace or tucked away inside the school building

Old Skool Academics	New Skool Academics
Memorized your times tables from 1-12	Show your math strategy to get the multiplication answer
Students physically attended school to earn graduation credits for diploma	Students can take credit recovery courses online if they fail a course; some complete 90 hours of community service to graduate and earn diploma
Reading was FUNdamental; students were taken to library weekly to pick out new book	Cell phones are mandatory; student melt down if battery is dead or phone lost
Webster's Dictionary, thesaurus and encyclopedias were key resources to learning new words and information	World Wide Web, Google, social media and Wikipedia can be unreliable or "fake news"
Gym time was the favorite class special and everyone participated (volley ball, kickball, crab soccer, dodge ball, basketball and gymnastics)	Lack of participation and inactivity (now physical education) has led to childhood obesity
Weekly spelling tests every week; 20 vocabulary words studied on student grade level	Spelling words taken out of school curriculum: (rite wright write)
Used dictionary and thesaurus to learn how to use "guide words" reading skill	Use computer spellchecker or Dictionary.com to pronounce word for you
Parents reinforced homework expectations to support academics learned in classroom	Parents complete student's homework and projects
Everyone passed Driver's Education; student saved to buy first used car	If student fails Driver's Education, parents must pay to retake; student still gets new car

Used No. 2 pencils	Use mechanical pencils
Stayed on campus to earn 4-year degree; share dorm with roommate & come home on weekends (campus ID required)	Stay at home; take online courses to earn degree (not certain who is completing the course for the student)
Parents signed tests, quizzes, report cards and exams to see grades and student progress. If child failed, teacher would automatically call home	Parents attend teacher conferences by appointment or go online to Schoology or HAC to review tests, quizzes, exams, and homework assignments. Teachers not allowed to accept phone calls in classroom during school hours
Parents were invited to the school any time to see teacher, eat lunch with student or help out in classroom or library	Parents are not allowed to visit the classroom unannounced
After reading a classic book on literature, wrote 1-2 page book report (Grades 3-12)	To avoid reading the entire book, rent the movie or read the Cliff Notes
All students participated in high school graduation practice and ceremony	Students can request diploma mailed to home address
School pictures were taken in the gym with a selection of one pose with limited sizes	School pictures offer a variety of season poses including key chains, keep sakes, and jewelry

Old Skool Behavior	New Skool Behavior
For excessive talking in class, mouth was taped; wrote "I will not talk when teacher is talking" 100 times on lined paper or on chalkboard	Student threatens to physically harm teacher; policeman with gun stationed on school site. Some schools have weapon checks at entrance
Unruly behavior or disregard to authority not tolerated in school; hands slapped with ruler or paddle on behind	Teachers cannot give corporal punishment to students; guns or weapons brought to school to harm teacher or students
On Christmas day, all children got new bikes and toys and played outside in winter	No physical activity outdoors on holidays; children nestle up to big screen T.V. playing latest video games all day and all night unsupervised
If school called home, behaviors would change with spanking and letter of apology	Spanking or physical contact for discipline is considered child abuse
Boys got haircuts and girls wore pony tails or plaits with ribbons; easy to tell student gender and bathroom signs	LGBTQ or transitioning: school must be notified that student can't use gendered bathrooms at same time with others; now students can be genderless
Anyone have the time? Look at wrist watch in Roman numerals with second hand (quarter past 4 or 15 minutes past 4)	Anyone have the time? Unable to read analog clock (with moving hands); only digital clock 4:15 (displayed numerical digits)
Able to count back bill change from merchant purchase ($1, $5, $10 or $20 bill)	Unable to count back change—extra penny/nickel with bill is confusing

I know that times have changed since you grew up and I still have fond memories of my childhood, too. But in today's world of education, teaching has changed over the last 100 years. Schoolhouses were built in the 1700's and have come a long way from 8-10 desks and meager supplies for learning. As schools continued to grow and universities were founded, the educational process became the foundation staple for families to move ahead for better paying jobs, taking care of their families and just building a better life.

Depending on the year you went to school, think of how:

- you were disciplined for behavior
- you spent time studying
- you were taught to learn
- many educational resources were available in your classroom
- some modern technologies were used during teaching (filmstrips were today's power point slides on a projector and cassette players were today's Audible on tape)

Computers stood as tall as a person and newer technology was still on the horizon or being invented. Having paper, pencils and a used textbook was the best some schools could offer.

When we look at school children today, they have all the latest technology, diversified teaching, advanced learning tools and curriculums that past educational frontiers could never imagine or fathom. "*New Skool*" education has reached record limits in our digital world and will forever change leaving the "*old skool*" as some might know it as the best education of our time.

Did you know that.......

.... 32 million Americans are unable to read to their child because they are illiterate or come from outside countries where English is a second language (ESL)?

....children aged 3-5 should read at least 1,000 books <u>before</u> starting kindergarten?

....summer reading is offered at your local library to increase literacy at an early age?

....the library staff offers read aloud and storytelling to young readers?

....children can earn free books and major grand prizes by logging their reading hours?

....child brain development is strengthened during summer months?

Your Turn Activity:

1. **Watch a classic T.V. show** Discuss with your child the differences between today's academics in the classroom and how teachers handled classroom management back then. How was discipline handled compared to today? Explain which works best and why.

Leave It to Beaver	What was Mrs. Landers like as a 3rd grade teacher? How did Ward handle discipline at school with his two sons? How was June's style of discipline different from Ward's'?
Father Knows Best	Were each of the 3 children on the same academic levels? How were they different? Why did Jim always consult with Margaret about school discipline? How did they handle disagreements?
Dennis the Menace	As an only child, why was Dennis always in trouble? How did Henry and Alice handle school discipline? Why was Dennis always over Mr. Wilson's house for advice?

2. **Find a few back in the day games** like jacks, paddle ball, marbles, tic tac toe and checkers. Why do you think these simple games were so much fun to play? How did it develop cognitive skills and hand/eye coordination?

Paddle Ball   Skill:____

Jacks   Skill:____

Checkers   Skill:____

Marbles   Skill:____

3. **Have your child write a summary about 3 of their favorite T.V. shows** See if they can get the main idea of the episodes and relate them to the real world. What can you do if the written summary is not legible?

Favorite TV Show (Pick 3 & write 3 summaries for each)	What is main idea? Was there a lesson learned?

Chapter 2 Notes

Chapter 2 Notes

CHAPTER 3

Step 3: Meet all proficiency levels in school
which determines yearly grade promotion.

Chapter 3

Common Core Standards: Report Cards Don't Lie

What is CCS and why do I need to know and understand each grade level requirement?

Reading the teacher comments on report cards gives an overview of student performance such as behavior, attendance, test scores and academic concerns to seek out academic resource support early.

What is a Report Card?

Do you remember your first report card in kindergarten? Even though you may have had front teeth missing and some wiggling on the side, it was important to have a good report to show mommy and daddy. If it was bad, then it was time for the dreaded Parent/Teacher Conferences at your school. It's really a *wake-up call to help struggling students in academics.* Here's an example of some of the Core Subjects listed on a report card:

In Elementary

- Computer
- English Language Arts
- Library
- Math (requires explaining answers in writing)
- Reading
- Science
- Social Studies
- Specials (Music, Art, Physical Education, Spanish)
- Writing

In Middle School

- Art
- Band
- Business
- English Language Arts/Literature
- Family & Consumer Science
- Foreign Language
- History
- Information Technology (Computers)
- Integrated Math (Algebra)/Geometry
- Physical Education
- Science/Biology
- Social Studies
- STEM (Science, Technology, Engineering & Math) Career Introduction/Exploration

- African-American Literature
- American Literature
- Biology
- Business
- British Literature
- Careers Exploration
- Civics
- College Prep Courses
- Cooperative School/Work Programs
- Driver's Education
- Earth and Space Science
- English I & II (Honors or AP)
- Family Consumer Science
- Foreign Language I & II
- Fundamentals of Finance
- Health/Physical Education
- Information Technology (Computers)
- Integrated Math I & II (Algebra)
- Introduction to Literature
- Performing Arts
- Visual Arts/Film
- Vocational Education
- World Literature

How Common Core State Standards and Report Cards Work Together

Common Core State Standards (CCS) measure how a student is performing at their current grade level and the report card is the gauge that determines end of year promotion. Each state has CCS but private schools are aligned differently.

The CCS was an initiative created in 2010 to help ensure that all students in grades K-12 could perform in English Language Arts and Mathematics by the end of their grade level which would prepare them for post education in college and enter the workforce. Each standard is a very specific combination of mathematical computations and concepts, reading and comprehending texts, writing distribution and final production while building on key concepts of scaffolding knowledge learned from grade-to-grade.

For example, let's take a reconstructed look at what a kindergartener must know in order to make it to first grade:

Kindergarten & Grade 1
How Grade Level Proficiency is Done

In reading text, a student must be able to:

- compose (write) an opinion about a book they read

- explain what they are writing about with details

- tell about the events in the order they happened

Now in the production of this writing piece, they will need help from an adult if they have to answer questions and even more guidance to read with them out loud what they wrote. The tricky part with writing is that if a student can't write their ABC's legibly or struggle with getting sentences together that make sense, parents, teachers and guardians **must help them practice** this cognitive skill on a daily basis on light green <u>lined paper</u> that looks similar to this:

Kindergarten teachers have the green paper with the red dotted line in the middle by the boat loads which is how they practice writing in the class room every day. They also know that since their little friends have such small hands, a big pencil helps them with grip. The alphabet is displayed all over the room as a reminder for what small and capital letters look like along with a picture that matches each letter so that they can repeat the sound it makes.

The alphabet song helps, too! But *remember, just because a kindergartener knows the song by heart, doesn't mean they know the letters when shown to them out of order.* Parents can open up the Report Card Packet and determine if their child is meeting mastery skill levels. It looks something like this:

Proficient	(P)	Child meets grade level
Near Proficient	(NP)	Child near grade level
Below Proficiency	(BP)	Child below grade level

Grade 2
Get to Know Classmates & The 7 Writing Traits

This grade starts to get more elaborate with writing details and explaining topics. They are still writing about opinions but now have to use linking words (*because, and, also*) which starts to connect their sentences. The standards look for conclusions and student development in the short written pieces. Also revising and editing is introduced by the teacher to help students review and recognize sentence structure and clarity. If students cannot perform this writing distribution, it will soon interfere with Grade 3 which requires even more knowledge of the 7 writing traits: I call it the **COW'S VIP.** When children think of COWS, they smile because they know a snack and milk (which is very important) is coming soon—especially if they worked hard and are doing their best to fight off that needed nap before the 3 p.m. school bell rings. The 7 Writing Traits break down something like this:

C= **Conventions**—include spelling, punctuation and capitalization

O= **Organization**—how can you get this story started?

W= **Word choice and vocabulary**—should be on grade level

S= **Sentence variety or writing fluency**—sentences become longer

V= **Voice**—narration and storytelling style at its best

I= **Ideas**—this goes with organization; brainstorming helps get this party started

P= **Production**—can be a story, letter, PowerPoint, book report; how it gets presented
to the audience

Grade 3
The Great Playground Yeller &
Story Teller of all Time

Third graders love to tell all their parents' business. They already know where babies come from (the grocery store). They talk fast and with a lisp because of loose or missing teeth. They are cell phone savvy, have the best hair dressers and barbers in the neighborhood, and the girls keep well-manicured nails with cute little hearts that I could never afford. The boys? Well, of course they always have the latest Lebron James sneakers money can buy.

For Grade 3 Common Core State Standards, students should be able to have some kind of prior knowledge or opinion as well as thought out reasons or explanations on certain topics given. These topics focus mostly on informational writing and should be elaborated upon with linking words (*also, more, but, and*) which summarizes a well-developed conclusion to show understanding of the topic introduced. Sentences should also be longer and grouped together, well organized, and developed to show topic relation and comprehension. Editing and revising along with parent and teacher guidance now involve using technology into their homework and project assignments which may include research, sources from print and digital, and their own opinions, thoughts and feelings about the world in which they live.

For parents, this is when school can be a good or bad experience for their elementary child. If the child learned and mastered the writing concepts in K-2, then he/she will be eager and ready to continue the writing process throughout middle school. But for many students, the hardest concept is *paragraph structure and the sentences that make it complete*. Here's a reconstructed example of what students write and interpret as a 3-sentence writing piece:

Line 1	The prisident of Amerka has and impashent jobe and help
Line 2	us wif healf karre problums too take care of or famlyz so
Line 3	I dont have to wury bout why nana go to the hospitul.

In reality, this student has **only written 3 lines** and believes that these are three good sentences. Most students <u>count lines as sentences</u> and become frustrated when they have to write more. It takes at least 3-5 sentences to form a good paragraph. By Grade 3, students should be proficient with writing *three* good sentences with punctuation and graduate to sentence variety and fluency to meet the Common Core Standards for writing 3-5 paragraphs by Grade 5. This process should begin on Loose Leaf lined paper and the *red line* on the left and right sides should now be introduced as the "imaginary writing margin." Students should also know how to write letters correctly (tall and short) and the 5 S's from Chapter 1 should now be reviewed for practicing writing legibility.

However, if students still are unable to …….

- write legibly on lined paper

- form complete sentences

- recognize missing punctuation

- capitalize letters at beginning of sentences and proper nouns

- use finger to indent and begin paragraphs

- read fluently and/or with expression

- comprehend basic stories and short articles

- comprehend basic instructions

- use punctuation to end sentences

……..then it is time to bring in a tutor or learning coach to review and practice these needed skills on a weekly basis. The report card will tell you everything you need to know about how to help your child academically. The teacher comments are very important and is a general guide to how your child is behaving in the classroom, gets along with others and how well they perform on tests, quizzes and standardized assessments. Teacher comments in the agenda book will also tell you what your child does on a daily basis. If he or she brings home gold starts and smiley faces then learning is fun and following directions and getting along with others will follow into the next grades.

However, if he or she brings home sad faces and continues not to follow directions or get along with others repeatedly, then it is time to meet with the teacher to find ways to improve classroom behavior or discuss other issues that may be going on at home.

Grades 4 & 5
What's Next?
More Non-fiction Text

In Grades 4 and 5, students are introduced to understanding various "*text structure*" while reading textbooks, articles, and newspapers or writing biographies, speeches and essays. Since this is "non-fiction text," it is also referred to as "informational text" which is really the short version of how our children understand the real world we live in. They are now introduced to understanding main ideas and finding details in what they read to make "**inferences**" or guesses based on what they found as "evidence" that backs up what they uncovered. As you can see, this grade is starting to prepare them for middle school and if a child cannot read on grade level, these concepts will become very frustrating throughout the rest of the school year. Here are the various types of text structure taught at this grade level:

- **Compare and Contrast**—authors show how two or more things are alike or different in a paragraph format

- **Cause and Effect**—authors show why things happen (the cause) and the result of what happens (the effect)

- **Sequence**—authors arrange things in time order (process, dates, steps, historical events, ages, etc.)

- **Problem and Solution**—authors introduce problems then encourage solutions to make it better

Along with understanding text structure, the Common Core Standards begin to **scaffold** in the areas of writing with a "point of view" which now encompasses Grades 1, 2, and 3 concepts. Can you see now how each grade Common Core Standard *must* be met in order to move along to the next grade level? This is why it is so important for students to keep learning during the summer so that they do not "forget" what they learned during the school year. In Grade 4 Common Core Standards, topics and texts will be introduced so students should now begin to **formulate** their own opinions, find the author's purpose for various types of writing (narrative, informative, persuasive, etc.) and provide reasons or support from the story to back up their evidence. The focus in this standard enables students to write *clearly* through use of transition words such as *for instance* using background information to show their development in comprehension of the topic. At this stage, other writing development will include knowing important details, character development and events, use of quotations, linking ideas into categories (*also, because*) and staying on the topic with beginning, middle and ending. Students should also be familiar with editing, revising and conventions of writing while using keyboarding skills to type up their final writing pieces. Researching and recalling information through digital sources will also be required to build prior and current knowledge along with the Reading Standards since reading and writing concepts build on each other. Now writing will require more sentence variety, longer paragraphs, detailed planning and organizing ideas to meet the required Common Core Standards while writing introductions, conclusions and headings or titles on a regular basis.

In Grade 5, many of the Grade 4 Common Core Standards will apply, but also include writing narratives (fantasy or real-life events), more variety of transition words and techniques that require quotations, vocabulary on grade level, and sensory details (see, taste, hear, touch & smell) to bring writing to life. Grade 5 is simply getting students ready for middle school English Language Arts (ELA) requirements and comfortable with the art of writing styles. This is organized structuring to explain, describe and sometimes analyze using their sense of logic and general observations about the world around us. When we think of author's purpose, students will support their point of view through various articles, newsletters, textbooks, illustrations, and overall information by using their learned vocabulary to explain it all based on their comprehension of the topic matter. They will also edit, revise and produce a final writing piece on a regular basis. This includes being able to sit longer periods of time, stay focused and write **at least one page.** Reading standards are also incorporated into these writing concepts since they build on each other in preparation for middle school adaptability.

Grades 6 & 7
State Your Claim:
Find Supporting Reasons to Aim

The whole idea of middle school is to continue building on the Common Core Standards of classroom instruction so that students can acquire the academic skills they need to reach grade mastery levels until graduation. They should continue to advance based on their prior learning and meet requirements to further develop as the Common Core Standards get more difficult into the high school level with stories, novels, fantasy, non-fiction and poetry. To show progress, here's what a sample report card could look like in Grades 6-12:

<table>
<tr><td colspan="3">ACCUMULATIVE GRADE LEGEND</td><td colspan="3">ABC Charter School
Your City, State 10330</td><td>School Year
1997-98</td></tr>
</table>

ACCUMULATIVE GRADE LEGEND				ABC Charter School — Your City, State 10330	School Year 1997-98

				Course	**Grade**	**Comments**
A=	92-100	OR	90-100	Science	81	5,7
B=	83-91		80-89	Math	63	10,12
C=	74-82		70-79	Physical Ed	94	3
D=	65-73		60-69	Social Studies	90	2
F=	0-64		0-59	English	79	6,12

Total Grade Point Average for MP2

81.444

Total Grade Point Average for MP1

75.678

MP 2 Absences: 5
Tardies: 2
Excused: 1
Unexcused: 6

Parent Note: Parent/Teacher conferences will be held on Thursday and Friday, October 20 from 8 a.m.-3 p.m. by appointment.

TEACHER COMMENTS

1=	has love for learning
2=	performs well on tests and exams
3=	works well in groups
4=	turns work in on time
5=	is not performing to ability
6=	frequent absences
7=	does not ask for help when needed
8=	behavior interferes with academics
9=	does not work well with others
10=	does not turn in work
11=	performs low on tests and exams
12=	request teacher/parent conference

In Grade 6, report cards are crucial since it is an accumulative progress report that measures a vast comprehension of subject concepts learned and mastered. It is also at this point that parents can make realistic assessments of academic levels of concerns as reflected by the teacher comments in the classroom and suggestions on resources for academic support on core subject areas of weakness.

Students will also rely on prior knowledge when introduced to new material such as *"claims"* and do their best to write clear reasons supported by evidence. Usually this is an **argument** that the author has introduced with given facts, background information, and drawn conclusions. Most times the topic will use strategies such as *comparison & contrast, cause and effect,* charts and tables and definitions or diagrams to help reader understand the content of the material. Often the **vocabulary** can be difficult if students are poor readers which makes comprehension a struggle in long passages. Now that they know what sensory details are from Grade 5, sensory language will be introduced especially in narrations, personal experiences and traits to show character development. Use of technology in the classroom will become more frequent to show real-world experiences along with keyboarding fluency (not hen-pecking) to produce a published final writing piece within a specific timeline. Now students will be expected to type *at least three pages* which requires an even longer sitting time. Also at this grade level short research projects will be introduced, gathering information from digital sources and totally *avoiding* **plagiarism** will be expected in their published writing pieces.

Grade 6 Reading Common Core Standards are also incorporated with regular routines of extended writing time frames. Editing, revising and proofreading are now required before turning in final draft assignments.

In Grade 7, everything learned in the Common Core Standards comes together for clarification in reasons and evidence. Now, **analyzing** becomes evident in the writing concepts and real-world topics along with reasoning, credible sources and evidence. Claims still take center stage, but now students must organize and understand the opposing claims in a logically way. Grade level vocabulary becomes relevant since paragraphs must be cohesive and show transitioning reasons to back up the evidence which can be located by going back in the text support. This becomes difficult for poor readers if they are not on grade level and comprehension becomes compromised. The Common Core Standards require clear and concise writing responses and specific vocabulary to express and explain these concepts. While students are expected to **paraphrase** their reflections and avoid plagiarism, they should work with a parent or adult to help them meet the writing **rubric** guidelines, especially literature that portrays historical texts or specific writing genre. Point of view, personal experiences, characterization, dialogue and other strategies will be reviewed to produce final writing pieces along with learned skills in editing, revising and proofreading. Research projects will also follow Reading Common Core Standards especially now in classic literature and novels. Students should develop stamina to sit longer to *type 3-5 pages* over the course of two days.

Grade 8
Can't Wait!
Playing it Technology Straight

Grades 8 encompasses all of the combined Common Core Standards from previous grades and continue to build on writing fluency, increased vocabulary, organizing ideas and comprehending even more information into broader categories. Students must now use "**technology**," especially the Internet to produce final writing pieces with reliable, credible sources while being able to work and get along with their peers in pairs, groups or independently.

Plagiarism is identified more carefully by the teacher and quickly corrected. Reading Common Core Standards become crucial at this grade level since selected stories can be from World, African-American, British, and European literature classics which require reading approximately *10-30* pages in a single sitting. Sometimes the Bible will also be introduced to show various religious themes, events or characterizations.

Since Grade 8 officially ends middle school, all writing development is expected to be mastered before entering into the high school grade levels. We now pioneer into the "real world" of college, career and workforce readiness.

Hopefully students who fell behind in elementary school have been identified to receive academic support from parents, counselors, teachers and tutors early on to help them navigate through high school graduation and beyond. Middle schoolers who have not mastered grade level standards will need extra academic support during the summer to retain important English Language Arts concepts and **remedial** practice to compete in the classroom and not fall behind their peers. Since many student athletes will play active roles in high school sports, this becomes a crucial transition in learning strategies in time management, study skills, academic review:

- in *Reading* (comprehension and author's purpose)

- in *Writing* (narratives, reflections, research papers, and conventions)

- in *Vocabulary* (recognizing words and meanings on grade level)

As grade levels become more difficult each year, students require increased stamina to sit for longer periods of time and transition from one core subject to the next in block periods (1 ½ hours or four classes each day) which require switching between classes (Periods 1,2,3,4 and 5,6,7,8) every other day in preparation for rigorous high school schedules the following freshman year.

Grades 9 & 10
Develop Clear, Concise, &
Analysis That's Nice

Grade 9 begins to focus on more complex information, ideas, connections and concepts using graphics and more technology through **multimedia**. Style and tone are introduced along with specific vocabulary that pertains to the main topic or idea. Hooking the reader is very important since that shows the use of writing strategies and techniques such as compare/contrast, **sequence**, and problem/solution. Being able to transition from one thought to the next is important when writing introductions, giving examples for ideas, or clarifying their knowledge in a selected topic. Grade level vocabulary is important since most topics must be developed from a real-world or fictional standpoint to show significance to the reader and audience. Stories and events may focus on characters, historical events, activities, or even **dialogue** interpretation.

Conclusions are also relevant to the production and distribution of writing because comprehension of the main idea must be concise and follow the **author's purpose.**

The Reading Common Core Standard in this grade focuses on analyzing literature, answering questions, **critical thinking** responses and understanding themes. Using vocabulary such as evaluate, identify, valid reasoning, and analysis must be clearly developed in writing since students are writing for even longer periods of time to combine for at *least 3-5 pages.*

Revising, editing and proofreading skills are expected in order to produce error-free assignments with the help of a parent, teacher or advisor. Technology will play a significant role in research, information queries, unfamiliar topics and how students present final projects (PowerPoint, videos, podcasts, blogs, designed websites, Google Docs, tri-fold posters, etc.)

Grades 11 & 12
English Language Arts & Kollege
Require Lots of Prior Knowledge

Prior knowledge is very important to college and career readiness in Grades 11 and 12. Writing arguments, finding valid reasoning, supporting claims and proving evidence is the gateway to entering higher education doors. All of the Common Core Standards introduce students to oral and written communication skills which help them meet college expectations for success. Here's how to gauge if a student has mastered the majority of the Common Core State Standards and can effectively demonstrate these Grade 12 level requirement strategies below:

- Write the definition of "biases"

- Write an effective reflective analysis

- Define the word "claim"

- Effectively explain "reasons"

- Find evidence in the text

- Explain the difference between *evidence* and *support*

- Recognize an author's purpose and explain why article was written

- Write clear and coherent enough to persuade any reader or audience

- Interpret complex ideas and concepts and simply explain to someone else

- Effectively write with style and tone

- Understand basic writing conventions and why they are important in writing

- Read, comprehend and explain main ideas in writing

- Use words, phrases and other syntax to convey point of view

- Read at the college text book level

- Effectively write a 5-10 page research paper using the rubric and assignment guidelines for reliable sources while avoiding plagiarism

- Communicate orally through explanations and descriptions to convey complex ideas and concepts to others

- Use appropriate vocabulary for First-Year College English Language Arts, Writing and Literature expectations

- Effectively use grammar, spelling, proofreading and digital formatting skills

- Read a 300-500 page novel in 1-2 weeks

- Use digital and technology skills effectively

- Write a reflection, analytical, or editorial paper and follow writing rubrics

- Understand the importance of historical events, U.S. Supreme Court decisions, constitutional principles and presidential speeches

This is a culmination of writing and reading concepts and strategies that students must master according to the state's Common Core Standards to meet graduation requirements. If more than three were not met from this list, a tutor and/or learning coach must be involved in your student's academic success. For parents, this is an opportunity to get involved in school parent/teacher conferences which are held each marking period to track academic progress. Your child's classroom work will be on display for your review as well as strengths and weaknesses in core subject areas.

Writing and reading go together like peanut butter and jelly and bacon and eggs. Eaten separately, they just don't have the same flavor. The Common Core Standards and curriculum synchronize like a well-oiled machine to position your child into the next grade level. When parents are involved in this educational recipe, it mixes together for a holistic education from kindergarten to college.

Did you Know that....

...the Common Core Standards have been implemented in 48 states to make it easier on families and children who move around in the military or other custody related reasons?

... National Handwriting Day is January 23 and students can enter a handwriting contest to compete for prizes and recognition in most schools?

...report cards are sent home in elementary school, but middle and high school parents can view report cards, assignments and missing work online with a password through a system called the Home Access Center also known as HAC?

...report cards are the key components to whether a student gets promoted to the next grade level?

...most middle school and high school students struggle to read a 300-500 page novel in a two week time frame?

...many students in grades 3 through 12 have developed handwriting that is not legible?

WORD of the Day: Methodology—branch of pedagogics dealing with analysis of subjects to be taught and the methods of teaching them

Your Turn Activity:

1. **Find your child's report card and look at the "teacher comments."** Is he/she meeting proficiencies or passing on their grade level? Write down the teacher's suggested comments.

Jane Doe's Report Comments	Your Student's Report Comments
(3) Pleasure to have in class	
(11) Easily distracted; wastes time	
(23) Low test scores	

2. **Time to take your Quiz!** Do you remember the 7 Writing Traits? Here's the acronym to help you get started.

C ____

O ____

W ____

S ____

V ____

I ____

P ____

(Answers on Page 61 and don't peek!)

3. **Think back to when you were in school.** What do you think was the hardest grade to pass? (Circle the grade(s) and explain why below.)

K   1   2   3   4   5   6   7   8   9   10   11   12

____

____

____

Chapter 3 Notes

Chapter 3 Notes

CHAPTER 4

Step 4: Practice how to read with expression; this involves comprehending and understanding what you have read to correctly answer response questions.

Chapter 4

This is Elementary, Dear Watson:
An Overview of Grades K-12

Who wants to be in the Readers' Theater classroom play?

Everyone except Billy who doesn't know how to "read with expression" and students who *can* read make fun of him because he is messing up the "theater" experience.

By now you've probably guessed that writing and reading go together. It's like pizza and hot wings. Chicken and dumplings. Grilled cheese and tomato soup. Cookies and milk. In this chapter you will learn that if it hasn't come together by Grade 3, the rest of the school experience will eventually begin to fall apart.

Here's what I want you to do. Read "My Summer Vacation" in this next section aloud to someone and ask them to time **(two minutes)** and rate you on the following:

- Fluency
- Rate or Speed
- Expression

Now, put your glasses on and get ready to read when the person signals and says, "Go!"

My Summer Vacation

Our trip to the beach was fantastic! At first, I didn't think we would make it, but after pestering my parents and convincing them that this would make lasting memories for a little kid, I knew I was a pro at manipulation. Who would guess that the ocean, the waves, and the sand castles on the beach with my family would bond us forever? The sun burn was worth it.

Now that school has started, I'm so glad that I saved that pail of sand memories in the trunk of our car. I sadly run my hands through it for motivation every time my teacher sends home third grade homework project assignments. Summer went by so fast that I blinked in June and the next thing I knew, "Back to School" commercials were popping up the first week in August! I'm glad we went to the beach and made lasting memories. Now, I've got to start thinking about our winter break trip and why we should create new white powder memories in Colorado....

Ok. If the person you read to fell asleep, then your invitation to "Story Time" at the children's library will be crossed off the list for next year. *Did you pay attention to the punctuation marks* in red? You probably noticed it half way through the story and wondered about it as you skimmed ahead. Children like being read to when the adult uses expression as they turn the colorful pages. Their eyes light up because the story teller raises and lower their voices, overacts the dialogue, pronounces each word with care, and can move quickly and smoothly through the text.

Let's rate your score for storytelling. (This is a good example of how students are scored on Reading Inventory text based on their grade level followed by 10 comprehension questions at the end)

YOUR STORY TELLING GRADE

(Poor)

Why didn't you put on your reading glasses *first* instead of trying to squint through the two paragraphs? By the time you noticed the red punctuation marks, it was too late and the story was not humorous or exciting as intended. With all those fumbles, you probably ran over your 2 minute time limit.

(Very Good)

You did pretty well on reading the story and understood the informational text! You skimmed ahead and noticed the red punctuation marks just in time to use expression and inflection as a story teller would. You may have missed a few punctuation marks, but your reader didn't notice since you finished honorably in 2 minutes. Good job, Captain Reader Underpants!

(Excellent)

Not only did you finish before your time was up, but your reader was so engaged that they called their parents to inquire about the next family vacation! You read so well that your next career could be with an audio books company. It was so smooth, so engaging and so exciting that the person in the other room came to see if the voice they heard was the television or radio. You were taught well at an early age that reading was important to being a good writer and oral communicator. Excellent job, Head Library Story Teller Extraordinaire!

Usually after a student takes the Reading Inventory like the one we just practiced, they answer at least 10 questions to check for comprehension. From the story you just read, see if you are able to answer the questions while someone reads the questions out loud and writes down your responses. *You cannot peek back at the story*! And you only have about 1 minute to think before you respond. If you don't remember, it will be marked with an "X" and then keep moving to the next question. Just respond, it doesn't have to be a long and drawn out answer. Do your best. You will be surprised at how much you will remember on short passages.

1. What was the title of the story passage? What was the author's purpose?

____

2. Where did the family go? How many people do you think went on vacation?

____

3. Name at least 3 activities the family did together

____

4. How old was the person who told the story? How do you know?

____

5. What is "bonding?" Why do you think it was important for the family?

____

6. When did school start back up?

____

7. Where was the pail of sand memories kept? Was this a good place? Why or Why not?

____

8. How does the person get through project assignments when school starts?

____

9. Where do you think the next family vacation will be? In which season?

____

10. Do you think the parents will agree to the next vacation? Why or why not?

____

Bonus: What is "white powder?"

Correct Answers____/10

Your Score: 9/10=A   8/10=B   7/10=C   6/10=D   5/10=F

SAMPLE Reading Inventory Comprehension Answers

1. **What was the title of the story passage? What was the author's purpose?**

ANSWER: My Summer Vacation. Author's purpose was to show how an elementary student could manipulate the family into a much needed vacation

2. **Where did the family go? How many people do you think went on vacation?**

ANSWER: Family went to the beach….family included mom, dad and the little boy or girl…..didn't mention any other siblings

3. **Name at least 3 activities the family did together**

ANSWER: They played in the ocean waves, built sand castles, got sunburned, bonded or shared conversations and were close (Any logical response)

4. **How old was the person who told the story? How do you know?**

ANSWER: An elementary school student between ages of 7-12…could be in first to fifth grade

5. **What is "bonding?" Why do you think it was important for the family?**

ANSWER: Bonding is sharing and doing things with each other…way for families to create lasting memories (Any logical response)

6. **When did school start back up?**

ANSWER: Soon since back to school commercials were coming on around first week of August, school might start in September or end of August

7. **Where was the pail of sand memories kept? Was this a good place? Why or Why not?**

ANSWER: Kept in back of car trunk…not good place because the pail could tip over or spill (Any logical response)

8. **How does the person get through project assignments when school starts?**

ANSWER: Goes to car and runs fingers through the sand to get motivation and remember good times on the beach….takes mind off assignments (Any logical response)

9. **Where do you think the next family vacation will be? In which season?**

ANSWER: Somewhere in Colorado to create winter memories in the snow

10. **Do you think the parents will agree to the next vacation? Why or why not?**

ANSWER: (Any logical response)   Bonus: White powder is snow

Correct Answers_____ /10   **Your Score:**   9/10=A   7/10=C   5/10=F
                                                    8/10=B   6/10=D

Fluency

Fluency is being able to read text with speed, accuracy and expression. It breaks down into three main parts:

- **Accuracy** is simply <u>reading words</u> without miscues or mistakes. Reading sounds so engaging, that is becomes just as natural as talking or having a conversation with someone in the room.
- **Prosody** is a big word that simply means that the <u>reader understands</u> <u>the text</u> and recognizes when to inflect expression. Reading is very *smooth* and at a good pacing speed.
- **Automaticity** is just like knowing when to brush your teeth in the morning and before bed. The **reader skims ahead and skillfully** *decodes words* *in the text without mistakes.* Decoding is another way of silently sounding out vowel or consonant sounds ahead of time to say the word correctly.

Comprehension

If you find yourself biting your nails or pulling your hair when a child reads, it generally means the he or she does not fully understand the content of informational text. They read in a droning or monotone voice, do not recognize punctuation at end of sentences, and struggle with decoding words which slows them down in their reading pace.

Rate or Speed

When a child can read fast, this usually means that they understand the text and like the story. They stop at punctuation, can act out the dialogue, and love reading in general. They mimic the person who read to them (who was probably a very good story teller) and more than likely was read to very often at an early age.

Expression

Not only is expression important in reading, but it keeps the attention of others when reading out loud. When children are poor readers, they don't feel confident reading in front of others. This is also true for adults, too. There's nothing worse than a poor reader trying to get through a passage, and others are making comments or clearing their throats or shaking their heads in disbelief. *Why can't they read with expression?* Why are they having trouble decoding or pronouncing words that are so easy to recognize? It seems simple but if the person was not taught early on it became a difficult task. This is why pre-school is so important when learning the alphabet, vowel sounds, and repetition of word walls so that vocabulary becomes automatic in reading. No wonder parents and teachers have to work together to ensure that students can read on grade level. Here's a reconstructed preview of some of the terminology used by Reading Specialists when they help create strategies for students to improve their reading fluency and word recognition:

Digraphs—group of two letters whose phonetic value makes a single sound together	br**ea**d, si**ng**, **ch**urch, **ph**one
Blending—two/**three** consonants that make single sound	bl, br, ch, cl, cr, dr, fl, fr, gl, gr, pl, pr, sc, **sch**, **spr**, sw, th**, thr**, tr, tw, **wh, wr**
Decoding—ability to sound out letters/ letter patterns and pronounce word correctly	Alphabet Consonants Vowels Definitions
Encoding—first stage of memorization; 2nd stage is memory storage 3rd stage is memory retrieval	Learning K-1 Sight words: we, can, family, you, us, the, our
Phonemes or phonemic awareness— knowing distinct sounds in beginning or ending of words	**bet, pad, pot, bat, dot**
Consonant sounds in alphabet **Silent consonants**	b, c, d, f, g, h, j, k, l, m, n, p, q, r, s, t, v, w, x, y, z **K**nife, **g**nat, **w**rist, **p**sycho, **h**erb
Sight words are generally recognized when seen in text **High frequency words** appear often in text	**school, because, important, family** **a, and, are, is, I, of, to, in, for, the**

There's more…..

Irregular words—cannot be decoded because sounds are unique or word not yet learned	colonel, yacht, Sioux, tongue, fuchsia, gauge
Vowel Teams	a, e, i, o, u (sometimes y) oi, ue, ee, ea, tion, oa, ie
Reading rate: Get word count for passage How long it took to read passage	100/5=20 wpm A passage of 100 words Read in 5 minutes= 20 words per minute
Diphthongs or **gliding vowels**; combination of two vowels that make one sound	**toy**, c**oi**n, l**ou**d
Literacy	Ability and knowledge to read and write
Syllables—pronouncing 1, 2, 3 or more sounds to form an entire word	syllable ice, freeze syllables wa/ter, ri/ver, o/cean 3 syllables mag/ne/tic, syllables dic/tion/a/ry, in/spir/a/tion syllables in/for/ma/tion/al u/ni/ver/si/ty
CVC words	Consonant/vowel/consonant Car, pet, did, mom, bus
Non-sense words vs. Real words	fiddle-faddle,humbug fickle farmer hamburger

Keep going….

Compound words—two words combined to make one word	understand, somewhere, milestone, skateboard
Vowel/Consonant— using both a vowel and consonant to make a word	is, at, or, am, an
Silent "e"	maze, stove, care, above
Reading Inventory Checklist	Main Idea Details Sequence Inference Cause & Effect Vocabulary
Dictation—reading words orally to be written	Spelling word list
down in order	Word definitions Notetaking Steps or process order
Controlled vowels	/ar/ car, far, are
Speech **Language**	art of talking sounds in the oral form of communication
Patterns **Rhymes**	jamboree, memory, mystery hike, bike, spike

As you can see, there's so much more to the reading process we've yet to learn! As basic as this seems, here's how it really starts in pre-school to college:

- Singing the alphabet song in correct order (From A-Z)
- Pronouncing the sounds the alphabet makes (M is mmmm)
- Distinguishing consonants from various vowel sounds (d, p, m, t) (a, e, i, o, u)
- Learning basic words from these letters (pet, dad, mom)

- Transitioning those words into sentences and reading correctly (My mom and dad gave me a pet.)

- Forming grade level sentence structure into organized paragraphs (beginning, middle, ending)

- Writing paragraphs that are logical based on given subject or topic

- READING <u>and</u> *comprehending main idea*

- Why we read and write (author's purpose)

Did you know that.........

...32 million adult Americans are illiterate and 14% of the population cannot read?

...newspapers are based on a sixth grade reading level?

...parents should read 1,000 books to their child <u>before</u> starting kindergarten?

...when children read their favorite books, they become better readers and love to read?

...summer reading programs are FREE at local libraries?

...many young students discontinue patronizing the library by the time they reach teen years?

...the library staff is trained to provide parent resources and services to parents and caregivers of young children?

...Delaware's Gov. Carney and Dolly Parton Imagination Library have collaborated to provide children one book each month from birth to 5 years old FREE of charge?

WORD of the Day: PHONOLOGY—study of speech sounds and sound system of a language

Your Turn Activity:

1. **Pick one of these classic stories below to read aloud to small children in the library:**

Three Little Pigs   **Little Red Riding Hood**   **Goldilocks and the 3 Bears**

When you are finished, ask their parents to rate you for "story telling" skills.

9-10   (Loud clapping and Hoorays!) Librarian has your story telling certificate

6-8   (Few finger snaps and better luck next time at another library)

3-5   (Children wandered off to the computers; parent glares)

0-2   (Not invited back; nana hit you on the head with her purse)

2. **Get a newspaper and locate the *Dear Abby* column.** Pick one of the letters to Abby and <u>read it out loud to someone.</u> After reading, see if the person can tell you the "**main problem**" in one sentence. Write down what they say below:

____

____

____

3. **In the same newspaper, locate the *Editorial* section.** Pick one of the letters and <u>read it silently to yourself.</u> After reading, see if you are able to **answer these 5 questions** below about the editorial without looking back at the editorial:

Who was this about? ____

What was this about? ____

Where did it take place? _______________________________________

When did this happen? ____

Why was this written? ____

Chapter 4 Notes

Chapter 4 Notes

Step 5: Learn how to critically write, think, analyze and orally communicate thoughts and ideas to others.

Chapter 5

Smack In the Middle: Middle School Blues

What do you want to be when you grow up? (Anything that makes a lot of money and requires little work)

Once halfway through the school year, it's time to render a true verdict on academic skills which will roadmap to a realistic career based on mental and physical behavior.

Middle school is called "middle school" for a big reason: this student population is smack in the middle of mastering elementary school, but not ready for the high school big leagues just yet. It's a form of psychology: parents perspire during their talks of where babies come from, why education is important, where babies come from, why you need to stay in school and more where babies come from—just in case they dozed off from the first lesson. They are growing rapidly and developing in places we didn't even dream of when we were that age. Some fifth graders could pass for ninth graders and the sixth and seventh grade boys can grow beards and fuzzy mustaches while the girls sprout overnight out of their T-shirts, skirts and mustard colored, ripped nylon tights. Yikes!

Even though they seem grown on the outside, if you truly listen to them communicate, you will hear some limited vocabulary language skills that project an awkwardness in group settings. This population yearns for attention and their cell phones are the primary and sometimes only link to their friends and social activities.

After all of their hard work to simply fit in, three years later they will soon enter into the high school arena and be at the bottom of the totem pole yet again in their academic journey. But, there is light at the end of this tunnel. Let's look at the skills required to make it during this time of difficult transition.

A New Way to Think: It's Quite Critical

When most people think of the word "*critical,*" they think of someone who has been injured in some sort of accident, taken to the hospital by ambulance and unable to move or talk which results in a severe and critical condition. On the other hand, we also think of the word "critical" as in judgement of how others see us. If the criticism is harsh, untrue or simply unjustified it can strain friendships, interfere with school, create misunderstandings in families and more.

In education, thinking critically involves claims, arguments, questioning, beliefs, evidence and not just taking someone's word that something or ideas are true. It's the ability to think things through and then being able to analyze facts, opinions and ideas for yourself. It's the ability to make up your mind about topics in today's world through other lenses known as biases, skeptics, prejudices, and speculations and then develop your own decisions about what is really true and not get taken advantage of by others.

For example, if someone says that you should only buy "new" cars, one could argue that it is also ok to buy a "certified used" car. A used car is less expensive, offers many of the same vehicle warranties and comes with choice of luxury upgrades. Though it requires a little more research, a person doesn't just have to accept the fact that he/she "has" to buy a new car. Now they can make a better decision and have an option based on their current finance situation leading to intelligent conversations with others. Without research, personal knowledge and experience, it becomes more difficult to engage with others on meaningful and real-world topics.

Critical Thinking in Reading

In reading, students come to a conclusion about the **author's purpose** and try to figure out why the author is declaring this **point of view** and why it matters. Next, they try to reason why the author feels this way and relate it to a real-life situation. This can be difficult for older readers, especially if the passages are long, the text font is small, and there are no pictures, diagrams or text structures to help them understand the main idea. To help us think critically, let's look at some purposes in which an author may write:

- To persuade

- To inform

- To entertain

- Historical facts

- To narrate

- To speculate

- Give an opinion

- To state an emotion

- Personal experience

Critical Thinking in Writing

In writing, students have to be able to put down their thoughts and ideas on paper using skills such as **analyzing**, describing, and reasoning. A significant part of written communication is how a student can express his or her thoughts in an organized way. If they cannot do so, then it will become increasingly difficult as they continue to navigate throughout their school career.

Ability to Analyze

Analyzing comes up in reading and writing and applies to all content areas in education. This skill appears as early as elementary school and continues throughout college and the workplace. Since analyzing involves "breaking things apart, thinking it through and breaking it apart again in small pieces," this skill is going to show up in many areas of a middle schooler's life such as:

- Resolving various problems, decisions or issues

- Buying the best product

- World news and media slants

- Health and wellness choices

- School and family life situations

- Deciding college or school to work

- Peer pressure

- Understanding relationships

- Cultural and diversity norms

Ability to Orally Present: You're Up Next!

Oral presentations are introduced as early as kindergarten when the teacher says, "Bring in something fun for Show and Tell." This was a quick assessment of how well children could express themselves in front of others. For middle school, it's "Career Day" and the student introduces their mom and dad while briefly explaining what they "think" they do for a living.

In high school, it's an "Oral Project" that might require students to read to an audience in order to receive a passing grade. As students near the end of their high school career, a Valedictorian or Salutatorian gives an anticipated "Graduation Speech" in front of hundreds of parents, family and friends.

Student leaders in clubs (Student Government Association (SGA), the school newspaper, teacher's assistants, etc.) will eventually present to demonstrate authentic oral communication skills to perform required job duties. As the presentation nears, here's a reconstructed sample of how a basic presentation rubric is scored below:

ORAL PRESENTATION SCORING RUBRIC

A= Excellent	B= Very Good	C=Developing	D= Poor	F= Fail
5pts. Stayed **on topic**, used examples, displayed enthusiasm; engaged audience	**4 pts.** Stayed on topic, used examples, displayed some enthusiasm; good attempt at engaging audience	**3 pts.** Did not stay on topic; used few examples and showed little enthusiasm. Attempted to engage audience	**2 pts.** Off topic; used 1 example and did not display enthusiasm— monotone. Little or No attempt to engage audience	**1 pt.** Off topic; no examples or display of enthusiasm— monotone. No attempt to engage audience
5pts. Maintained **eye contact** with audience throughout presentation	**4 pts.** Some eye contact with audience throughout presentation	**3 pts.** Very Little eye contact with audience throughout presentation	**2 pts.** Little or no eye contact with audience throughout presentation	**1 pt.** No eye contact with audience throughout presentation
5 pts. Loud and clear **voice;** advanced use of topic vocabulary	**4 pts.** Loud and clear voice; good use of topic vocabulary	**3 pts.** Inconsistent voice levels; little use of topic vocabulary	**2 pts.** Low or Soft voice/unable to follow along; little or no use of topic vocabulary	**1 pt.** Unable to comprehend dialogue/ hard to follow along; no use of topic vocabulary

5 pts.	4 pts.	3 pts.	2 pts.	1 pt.
Excellent/ Clever Poster Display, Power Point Graphics, or Project Creativity; 0 Spelling Errors	Very Good Effort on Poster Display, Power Point Graphics, or Project Creativity; 1-2 Spelling Errors	Attempted Effort on Poster Display, Power Point Graphics, or Project Creativity; 3-4 Spelling Errors	Little Effort on Poster Display, Power Point Graphics, or Project Creativity; 5 or more Spelling Errors	No Effort to complete Poster, Power Point or Project; If submitted, could not follow or understand

Logical Reasoning: Does it Make Sense?

Ask a middle schooler where babies come from and it will be much different from what a kindergartener would say. Some were told an actual "stork" (a big, scary white bird smoking a cigar) brought the baby to every neighborhood front door. After all, the stork sign was displayed on the front yard lawn (this helped with mix-ups) and when a newborn baby was delivered, the stork rang the doorbell and waited with the baby in its beak swaddled in a diaper until the happy parents greeted him at the door. A giant bird flying with a little baby made perfect *logical sense* and proved relevant to the Scooby Doo Mystery: *where do babies come from*? This reasoning could really be explained and answer all of the major questions to support this claim with the following information:

- **Data:** date of birth and weight provided on sign

- **Evidence:** a baby room (pink or blue) prepared in advance; gifts, food and child rearing advice followed shortly after each stork delivery

- **Evidence:** wails and demands upset household every two hours

- **Research:** mother's basketball stomach was magically gone; frequent doctor's appointments every 6 weeks

- **Relevance:** gained tiny new member of family with same last name

At this stage, middle schoolers begin to develop logical reasoning for anything that happens in their lives. They find accurate data (from the newest i-Phone), can agree or disagree with a topic of interest (through personal experience, hearsay or social media persuasion), and think credible sources are found on the Internet (sometimes fake news). When asked if they read a newspaper or occasionally watch television trusted sources as ABC, CBS, NBC or 60 Minutes the answer was simply, "No, I do like to read or watch boring shows." But in reality they are reading constantly! Looking down at a cell phone 24 hours a day is a lot of work. Ask a middle schooler if they can live without it, and we already know the answer. They sleep with it turned on next to their bed so that they can respond if someone, anyone sends them a text message. In their middle school minds, this is exceptional logical reasoning and the very best in cell phone best practices.

Group Participation

This is another skill that starts as early at kindergarten and later becomes crucial in middle school. The teacher says, "Okay ladies and gentlemen. Please get into groups of three and select a slip of paper in this basket." This is really the NASCAR signal for middle schoolers to scout out the best people in the class who have good organization and strong academic skills. Popularity reigns in the classroom as students quickly go to the person who is known to do well. After all, if these students are true over achievers, so will my final grade by hooking up! Participation becomes stressful early on and those students who aren't picked will stand out or feel left out of this group process. Teachers are in tuned when this happens and quickly intervene by matching and mixing up learning styles for the betterment of the overall group experience. Middle school is the beginning of developmental group projects and getting along with others to problem solve and formulate plans together to understand the expectation of this important collaboration skill. It will serve its purpose as they ready for high school, college and the real-world.

Balancing School and Sports: Time Management

What can you do in 24 hours or 86,000 seconds in a day? Everyone gets the same amount of time but what's really important is *how we spend it.* For middle school athletes, this is a tough skill to acquire since it will be their first exposure to juggling more responsibilities. Sports and academics go together like Gatorade and Nike sneakers. If you forget one or the other, there's no need to attend practice. Parents and coaches realize this and collaborate together to help young athletes develop time management in school work and after-school sports practice.

Every middle schooler I've tutored thinks an *agenda book* is lame. Why not just keep everything on their cell phone? After all, it has an elaborate calendar, reminder chimes, alarms, electronic bells and train whistles that most of us didn't even know existed on these electronic devices. But they know! Why do you think we go to them to help us find the flashlight, how to take a screen shot and why the notification sound keeps going silent on our phones? But here's the game changer: if the cell phone battery life is dead or they forget or lose the phone, *none of these technology advances can produce the science test notes needed in time for the science test coming next period.* The genius who is studying handwritten notes from the last six classes has the advantage to passing the test. Sounds antiquated I know, but **note taking** still exists in our modern day world along with neon colored high lighters, sticky notes and messy handwriting scribbles which make reviewing the science notes more authentic.

Get Organized:
Stop Being a "Pro" at Procrastinating!

Being organized is also the key to successful time management. What does Serena Williams (World Tennis Champion), Michael Jordan (NBA legend), Dale Earnhardt (NASCAR legend), Tiger Woods (Golf Champion), Elena Delle Donne (WNBA MVP) and Jackie Robinson (MLB Hall of Famer) and Muhammad Ali (Heavyweight Champion Boxer of all time) all have in common? **They are people who believed in being great at an early age and worked hard to be the best at their chosen sport.** Serena was hitting the tennis ball at over 40 m.p.h. at 9-years old. Tiger could swing the gold club at 3-years old. Jackie proved his talent and survived racism and prejudice in the early major leagues. Muhammad was in the boxing ring in his teens and knew then he was destined for greatness.

Notice that the above professionals are referred to as "pros" which also appears in the word **PROcrastinate**? Funny thing, they were destined to be great and most knew from a young age and pursued it until it became a reality. On the other hand, middle schoolers are very good at being "pros," too but many have become *professional* procrastinators in dodging homework, assignments and projects. They are so good that they sweetly convince their parents with a straight face to believe that all school projects are completed, class assignments are turned in on time, field trip slips do not require money or parent signatures and (here it comes) their room has been spot-cleaned, too.

Just wait until you pry open their bedroom door and find the half-done project in back of the dresser bureau, field trip slip in a jeans' pocket crumbled up in bits from the washer, and a room so smelly and messy that you step on some once life form of a moldy sandwich. As your eyes dart around the child's room, the computer glares the "missed due date" e-mail reminder to check **HAC**, the $15 field trip permission slip on the floor and the mandatory parent meeting flyer (which is tomorrow) requesting your attendance for middle school chaperones going to the fun-filled day at the aquarium. Oh, and you'll be riding on a bumpy, hot and crowded bright yellow school bus for two hours with an excited group of bouncy *student hormones*. Yay!

Controlling Behaviors (Mentally and Physically)

There's nothing more frustrating than dealing with angry students and trying to keep other students safe, which is the teacher's main concern when working with a Public Behavior System (PBS) usually put in place by the Student Dean. In middle school, administrator's know all the "here we go again" students because they are often the topic of conversation in suspension, expulsion or extreme behavior cases discussed in the staff social work or psychologist meetings.

If a student is absent most of the school year, this leads to truancy and termination from school with recommendation to an alternative school or juvenile detention center, pending on behavior. So what happens if a student physically harms another student, teacher or staff member? In some inner city and urban schools, police officers are stationed and armed on site. Some weapons that have been brought to school are "fake" guns, homemade butcher knives, snub-nosed pistols, semi-automatics and threats with "fake" bombs found in the school. One middle school I taught, we had 6 bomb threats in a school year! We stood outside for hours in the freezing cold as they finally caught the student calling on a cell phone using a fake name and disguised voice reporting the bomb threat simply by tracing the number. They found the student hiding in the hall closet with a friend who both thought it was a clever joke. Both were charged with a misdemeanor crime.

In other instances, I've witnessed students pull fire alarms for fun causing the school population to stand outside in the dead of winter or sweltering heat while firefighters collaborate with administrators to find out if there is a legitimate fire. The end result? A hefty fine for each false alarm. Some schools have reported up to five false alarms in a single school year.

What about bullies? They exist in the school and their behaviors and daily attendance to school are a growing concern. Their victims end up hurt, hospitalized or some commit suicide if the situation was not addressed early on. These new bullies now threaten the teacher, administrator or the policeman on site. They don't seem to be afraid of authority and when confronted, deny any wrong doing. It takes the school staff to document each incident and monitor ongoing behaviors in the classroom, playground and any incidents that take place on the school property.

Middle school is a brief pit stop where students develop character, integrity and hindsight to begin preparation for a life-long career to take care of themselves and a future family. They might be physically taller, stronger and appear much bigger than some adults, but you will know them by their level of maturity, vocabulary, problem solving, public speaking abilities, prior knowledge and exposure to personal experiences. When these areas are focused upon early, students acquire certain characteristics that help them navigate successfully or unsuccessfully through high school and college academic expectations.

Did you Know that.....

…public libraries recommend that students read 500 books **before** middle school to improve vocabulary and reading comprehension?

…238 million people (adults) are afraid to orally present in front of an audience?

…1 out of 5 people are chronic procrastinators?

…student athletes develop better time management skills while balancing sports and academics?

…most middle school students have a general idea of whether they will attend college, the armed services or go from school to work?

…behavioral problems in the middle school classroom usually result from students who perform three to four grade levels behind their peers in reading, writing and math?

…school bullying starts as early as Grade 1 and can go unnoticed if the student does not tell a parent, teacher or adult?

WORD of the Day: PSYCHOLOGY—the science of mind and behavior; the mental or behavioral characteristics of an individual or group

Your Turn Activity:

1. **Get 5 Post-It notes, then:**

   Write down 5 topics of your choice on each note
   Find 5 people (including yourself) and select a note
   Each has 5 minutes to orally present their topic using prior knowledge
   Rate each person on their presentation out of 5 stars:

5=Excellent & Engaging   4=Very Good   3=Fair   2=Rambling   1=Off Topic

2. **Use your critical thinking skills and respond to these opinions below:**

What you heard…..	Your response……
She said….. "I really liked the Obama Care program. Now that it's gone, none of us can pay our deductibles or see our doctors to stay well."	**You understand that….**
They said….. "The news described prisons over crowded. We need to put executions back on the top of our list to solve this world-wide problem."	**You believe that….**
He said…. "You don't need an education. There are jobs that don't require college degrees, pay well and offer job security."	**You think that…..**

3. **Sometimes emotions get the best of us. Tell of a time when you reacted and later apologized for your behavior.**

At home ____

At work ____

At a public place _______________________________________

Chapter 5 Notes

CHAPTER 6

Step 6: Know most literary terms, figurative language and basic types of writing genres (narrative, persuasive, informative, editorial/opinion, research, essay, and text response).

Chapter 6

Freshmen & Sophomores: Now requires writing much, much more

Are you writing and performing at grade level?

My mom's grocery list was a mile long. *(hyperbole)*
I was so hungry that I could have eaten a horse! *(exaggeration)*
As we circled each aisle, the cart danced around the store. *(personification)*
I was out like a light *(idiom)* by the time we got home.

Most freshmen and sophomores have taken the PSAT or ACT exam and know their scores in Reading, Writing and Math. In the classroom, the assignments are getting longer and students are expected to write more fluently. Some students are in English AP classes or Honors Classes to gain college credits early and get a head start in their field of study. For other students, regular high school courses can be taken and required to graduate high school. Here's an overview of the ***basic types of writing*** most familiar in many classroom assignments:

- Narrative
- Persuasive
- Informative
- Editorial
- Essay
- Research Paper
- Response to Text
- Outlines
- Personal Letter
- Book Report
- Comparison & Contrast

Here are some types of writing genres:

- Mystery
- Fantasy
- Romance
- Historical
- Western
- War
- Travel
- Science Fiction
- Financial
- Technical
- Stage Play
- Horror
- Non-Fiction
- Movie Scripts
- Interviews

- Memoirs
- Broadcast Journalism
- Newspaper
- Poetry
- Song Lyrics

Narrowing It Down:
The Narrative

Most freshmen I've taught dislike writing. Most sophomores follow the same suit. Most middle schoolers hate to write. Even kindergarteners don't like the evil task of writing their name because the alphabet is still a little squirrely: their **s's** are backwards while **b's**, **d's**, **p's** and **q's** really are the same in their alphabet book. So to narrow this down to a 9th and 10th grader mentality, their ultimate task and goal is to write a narrative paper in roughly one paragraph; two pages are out of the question.

They've done this before: *write about your summer vacation*. They simply tell the story from their perspective and give it an introduction, body (ideas and examples) and wrap it up in the conclusion. The hardest part is the topic. If it is not interesting, it will be the longest English class ever. If it's of interest, it will be the best English class ever. The key is writing for sentence variety, choosing appropriate vocabulary (word choice on grade level) and making the narrative interesting for the audience which is generally the poor teacher.

There are other types of writing that will be required at this level which is why the more they write, the easier it becomes to generate more topics of interest since they will eventually write for longer periods of time to develop research papers, create analytical responses and news worthy **rhetoric.**

By Any Means Necessary:
Persuasive Tactics

This group has a knack for persuasion. They have a reason for everything and can pitch it to anyone who will listen. This works particularly when they want something or have been told that they can't have it. English teachers love reading persuasive papers because student methods actually work! At this stage, they have gained enough prior knowledge to use **pathos, logos and ethos** very well. They have been exposed to television, social media and get a new i-Phone every time the latest version comes out. This technology allows them access to anything on Google and helps them learn faster than the teacher can introduce it in the course curriculum. Their views depend on how they were raised and how they get along in the world around them which reflects by any means necessary how they write.

Real News vs. Editorials

What's considered real news these days? For most of us it is any news that comes on ABC, NBC or CBS reported by live telecasters on the 5, 6 or 11 p.m. news feeds. It sounds real and is reported in real-time and every hour it runs again on every local news channel on television. Editorials appear in the newspapers and are told by real people with real opinions about the latest news reported in our communities. Teachers, attorneys, pastors, youth groups, retired veterans, politicians and many others have the opportunity to write their opinion of what goes on around our neighborhoods and how it effects our cities, states and the nation. From high gas prices to solar energy to our current President, everyone gets to tell their viewpoint in written format for others to review, comment or simply lend a listening ear. Freshmen and sophomores also get a chance to share their views in analytical responses and written summaries of stories, articles and world news in the classroom. Like all writing genres, the <u>more they write the more they will be able to prepare for</u> <u>college courses and eventually the workforce</u>.

Let's Get Personal:
Writing a Personal Letter

When I taught middle and high school, many of my students didn't know the 5 parts of a letter. I was shocked and realized that I had to reteach the concepts and of course practice writing a personal letter and reasons why we write letters in the first place which included:

- Office and Business (inter-department mail, staff and administration)

- Personal (friend, family or relative)

- Grievance (problem or situation)

- Refund request (merchandise, product or service)

- Employment (termination or reference)

- School (health, meeting, reports, textbooks, data, etc.)

- Customer Service (thank you, recommendation, etc.)

Here are the 5 parts of a basic one-page personal letter:

1. DATE **February 11, 1995**

2. SALUTATION **Dear Mr. Cannon:** (Include colon)

3. BODY **One to five paragraphs about the reason you are writing this letter**

4. CLOSING **Sincerely,** (Include comma)

5. SIGNATURE **Your name signed in cursive**

Essay you Say...
Do we Have to Write One Today?

Essay formats are crucial writing strategies for freshmen and sophomores since it prepares them for the college application process and admissions. In the classroom, essay writing is not the favorite since it requires prior knowledge of the following:

- Brainstorming a topic

- Generating ideas and examples for support

- Developing a hook for the introduction paragraph

- Building body paragraphs that are organized

- Constructing a good conclusion based off the introduction

- Demonstrating strong word choice based on grade level vocabulary

- Incorporating transitional paragraphs that tie main ideas together

In order for students to master essay writing, *practice is the key*. A major component is a variety of subject matter in all areas of science, math, technology, space, education, medicine, sports and more to instill **prior knowledge** of these areas throughout their high school career. Students who can engage in many areas of interest can benefit them in writing college essays since they are asked to recollect areas of prior knowledge to express their thoughts when comparing or analyzing time periods using examples based on their own life experiences.

Textbook responses: Not a Cell Phone Text

Since many schools are choosing online textbooks, it's becoming more and more difficult for students to actually feel and turn the pages of an actual textbook. They would rather look at their cell phones (tiny screens) than view a full sized 8 ½ x 11 hard cover book, especially high school literature books that feature short stories, vocabulary introduction and practice questions at the end of each unit. Literature books are unique in that they focus on areas of writing, grammar, response to text, summary practice, story comprehension and exposure to other cultures and civilizations. Literature also opens a student's mind to analyze, evaluate, infer, predict and explain their reasons based on the evidence found in the story and use these events based on their own personal experiences. Since textbooks are used across the school curriculum, students are expected to write in all courses which helps in college and workforce preparation. Students who can engage in many areas of interest introduce themselves to the types of literature written by world renowned authors of British, American, World and African-American works which contributes to even more knowledge through poetry, realism, romanticism and modernism periods that are crucial to knowing key events in our history.

What are Literary Terms?

Throughout elementary, students will be introduced to **literary terms** as long as writing is a part of the school curriculum in English Language Arts. These terms begin with developing a sentence in first grade to the last research paper in their senior year. Once students begin to read, the story elements open up to inspire a love for reading even more from leveled readers to chapter book novels capturing their imagination for longer periods of time. Here are a few basic literary terms students will have heard and learned to use in writing:

Elementary

- Characters—people or animals who participate in the story
- Story—involves characters and a main idea that sometimes includes a problem
- Fable—a tale told to teach a lesson or moral; usually involves talking animals
- Tall tales—an exaggerated story humorously told about supernatural main characters
- Imagery—using the 5 senses to describe sensory details (see, taste, hear, smell, touch)
- Rhyme—same sounds of two or more words (name, game, same)
- Setting—time and place of story

Middle

- Metaphor—comparison between two unlike things yet they have something in common
- Simile—uses "like" or "as" to compare
- Irony—using contrast in reality; opposite of what it appears to be
- Figurative language—ideas that go way beyond literal meanings; usually called figure of speech (example: simile, metaphor, hyperbole, personification, idioms, etc.)
- Fantasy—uses fiction to imagine events, characters and setting that is usually unrealistic in the real world
- Plot—order of events in a story (follows exposition, rising action, climax and falling action)
- Climax—reader reaches the turning (or highest) point in the story
- Exposition—problem or situation in early part of story
- Point of view—how a story is told (first, second or third person)
- Dialogue—conversations between characters that take place in story or novel

High School

- Satire—ideas or customs are ridiculed or made fun of
- Epic—usually long poetic narrative describing adventures of a hero through good and evil
- Personification—human qualities are given to objects or ideas
- Protagonist—main hero in story
- Types of Characters—flat, round, static and dynamic
- Antagonist—can be more than one villain in a story
- Short story—shorter than a novel or chapter book
- Soliloquy—character says thoughts out loud; usually away from other characters
- Sonnet—a poem of 14 lines; common in Shakespearean works
- Voice—writer uses own personality to give writing characteristics heard by the reader
- Hyperbole—an exaggerated truth used for emphasis or humor

Literary terms are an important part of the school's English and Writing curriculum and will carry into first-year college. For freshman and sophomore students, this is a crucial time to learn, understand, and become familiar with how these terms are used since they have been introduced in early elementary and continue to build upon writing and reading concepts throughout high school.

What happens when freshmen and sophomores dislike reading and writing more than a paragraph and struggle through homework time each night at the dinner table? Every parent goes through this phase at one time or another and it has to be addressed sooner than later. At this stage, students are glued to i-Phones and live in a "text me" world downloading videos and apps, watching YouTube, facetiming, video conferencing, talking to Google and ordering food from GrubHub 24 hours a day. Everything is within technology reach or a simple voice command which takes away from any type of creativity in thinking, decision making and finding out information on their own.

An important reality is that *reading and writing really do go together* and later develop into ideas on paper which prepares students for the college experience or workforce. When a student lacks proficient written and oral skills to communicate effectively, it becomes difficult in the classroom to perform on grade level. This sets the tone for college readiness and shows proven skills learned during college admission testing. If scores are below the College 100 level, students will enter into **remedial** English and Reading courses until they are ready to perform at the college requirement and meet prerequisites in the classroom.

For some first-year students, it could take several years to complete remedial courses which delays and interferes with their overall graduation rate.

To avoid this unnecessary process, skills must be mastered early on and grades should remain consistent while in the 9th and 10th grades. Some students do their best to communicate with their teachers in written format to get help with assignments, report a problem or concern or take leadership roles to be the spokesman of a group. Either way, written communication is the foundation to the beginning of the writing process.

Here's a reconstructed example of a high school freshman trying to communicate to a teacher through e-mail. See if you can:

- understand the concerns regarding the project assignment

- find the grammatical errors and incomplete sentences

> Hi, Mrs' ___________________________
>
> I've been Schooloy. Need to see rulbric and why talk to dress up. Failing our group not doing there part so can do by myself. Started powerpoint sliding.

In case you couldn't understand the e-mail, the student *was asking the teacher for group mediation on the project, how to locate the project rubric on Schoology, why the presentation required dress code business attire, and gave an update on the PowerPoint slides.* In the real world, most teachers require at least 48-72 hours to respond and some prefer to respond in person to avoid confusing the situation altogether, especially if the e-mail is difficult to read and does not include punctuation, capitalization or make sentence sense. As a rule, a student e-mail should always include:

- student's first and last name

- subject title (English 101)

- class time and period (Period 1 at 10-10:50)

- today's date

Let's try another reconstructed e-mail to the teacher from a high school student in Grade 10. The date was supposed to be 2017:

Hey Mr. ________________________________   Oct 3; 2071

I am not able to due the class because im going on a trip with moms and wont be backward in time. You heard my voice before so you shouldn't take pints off. Can I take up miss work? Tell my peeps hey.

In this e-mail the student *did not complete the required presentation because of a weekend trip and wants to make it up upon his return.* When teachers give specific assignments, they are usually spelled out in the course syllabus and expected to be completed when the due date is given. Unless you have a valid excuse, the teacher may use their own discretion in how this situation is handled. For most students, it's important to talk to the teacher in person (not through e-mail) as soon as you learn of the problem or situation. This shows concern and responsibility on your behalf which gives a better chance of leniency and collaboration with the teacher since real-life events and unforeseeable circumstances can arise.

Furthermore, some teachers are responsible for several course subjects so when sending e-mails be sure to include pertinent information to help them locate and respond to the correct student. Most high school students do not know that at the university level, class sizes can be up to 75-300 students in a single lecture hall which offers over 50 course and degree programs each semester. So, if a high school freshman or sophomore needs help with written communication or completing assignments and projects for their teacher, try these suggestions for a better academic outcome:

a) find another teacher or tutor to proofread the e-mail <u>before</u> you send it

b) make a trip to the English or writing lab for academic support

c) meet with your teacher after class or school for clarification on assignment and project expectations (write down questions before you meet)

d) ask teacher for help navigating Schoology to locate important information (take notes so you'll know what to do after you leave)

e) find a classmate to buddy and study with each week; compare notes and work on projects together

f) begin project same day of class; work backwards from the due date (share with teacher to make sure you are on right track)

g) find out how much projects (or missed assignment points) weigh on your final grade

h) don't assume that assignments or projects can be made up; check with teacher for clarifications and rubrics

Classroom Size Matters
Public vs. Private Schools

Teachers who have up to 35 students in their classes do not have the convenience of going back in the curriculum to reteach writing and reading skills that should have been mastered in the grade before. Each skill builds on the last concept (or **scaffolds**) taught and if it is missed, that student can easily fall behind. At this grade level, all skills lead up to the next grade and the teacher does his or her best to meet most of the required Common Core State Standards and can measure mastery through quizzes and chapter test scores. For students with education disabilities, a team of special education teachers put together an **Individual Education Plan** (IEP) with very specific accommodations and then monitor academic progress each year for mastery.

This plan also follows the student through college and it becomes a **Student Education Plan** (SEP) monitored and enforced by the Admissions Advisory Team. These plans are mandatory implemented through the state and become official educational documents of law. Violators are prosecuted and faculty and staff are held accountable for carrying out its yearly updated instructions and accommodations for each student.

With so many students in the classroom and a ratio of about 35:1(in public schools) or 20:1(in private schools), teachers are easily frustrated trying to maintain and monitor curriculum goals to meet Common Core State Standards in each subject. Parents and guardians play a major role in their child's homework, grades and discipline which helps the teacher and parent collaborate all year long to ensure academic accountability and progression into the next grade level. Reading and writing are basic fundamentals that continue to build in strengthening written communication skills, improved vocabulary and oral communication. So when students say they dislike to read, it should be addressed immediately. Here are some reasons given below:

- Reading too slow

- Vocabulary is below one, two or three grades below reading level

- Reading without expression; not recognizing punctuation signals

- Unable to comprehend what was read

- Unable to find evidence or support in the text

- Peers make fun or laugh when they are called on; labeled as poor reader

With high school graduation just a few years away, it's important for freshmen and sophomores to understand why these grade levels are so important.

Everything that they learn going forward is based on what should have been mastered in elementary and middle school. Teachers will continue to do their best to cover the Common Core Standards for each grade level, but it's the student and parent responsibility to remain accountable for the information taught, content matter studied and unit test/exam mastery reviewed.

Want to Build Strong Reading and Writing Skills? Get to the Library Down the Road and up the Hill

If you leave it up to a freshman or sophomore student, many will *never step foot in a local library again.* To them, it's <u>so elementary</u> and they would rather sit in the car than hang out in the teen book section, read a local newspaper or pick up one of 100 magazines on display. In reality, the library is the best place for them to hang out to gain exposure on thousands of books and community happenings unfamiliar to possible social interests. Since most high schools have libraries, students already know that they exist and are encouraged to check out books, explore scientific journals and learn the basics of general research to increase their knowledge of how to find information that is "real" and not fake news.

For some students, it will take years to build strong reading fluency and continued practice to stay focused on topics they think are boring or a major waste of time. As they continue to prepare for college readiness, they have to accumulate **reading stamina** in various stages:

- Small news articles (1-4 pages)

- Short stories (3-10 pages)

- Chapter books (60-200 pages)

- Classic novels (up to 400-600 pages)

Although reading stamina happens over time, students can start right away in their classroom through required reading assignments, book reports, ELA projects, and finding a favorite book or novel on their grade level. And to increase their interest in reading, parents can introduce them to browsing newspapers published from different states (*Baltimore Sun, Philadelphia Inquirer, New York Times and Wall Street Journal, The Trentonian, etc.*) and then mosey over to the magazine section which offers 50 or more genres from art to zoology ready to be explored on the library shelves.

Did you Know that...

…40-60% of students are not college ready and enter their first-year at the remedial level?

…low-level students with Student Education Plans (SEP) could take as long as 2-3 years before starting at college level-100 courses to earn their degree?

…students who have Individual Education Plans (IEP) in high school receive free academic support and tutors in college?

…some public school classrooms can be an overwhelming 40:1 ratio when a teacher is absent and substitutes do not show?

…some high schools allow athletes to participate on sports teams with a 1.75 G.P.A. or less?

…many high school athletes do not meet NCAA first-year college requirements to participate on a sports team?

….some schools have had their student library and media resources funds cut from the school curriculum leaving unused books and textbooks in abandoned storage?

WORD of the Day: LEXICOLOGY—Linguistics; study of the formation, meaning and use of words

Your Turn Activity:

1. **Write an imaginative poem** that tells a story and rhymes with these end stanzas:

____ **sight**

____ **delight**

____ **weather**

____ **feather!**

2. **Name at least 5 types of writing genres below:**

____

____

____

____

____

(Answers on Page 110…No peeking!)

3. **Do you watch the television news?** Explain why or why not. What do you define as "real news" and "fake news? Give some examples below:"

I watch the news because ____

I do not watch the news because ____

What I think is **REAL** News	What I think is **FAKE** News
1.	1.
2.	2.
3.	3.
4.	4.

Chapter 6 Notes

Chapter 6 Notes

Step 7: Confirm all graduation requirements, pass English and read on grade level for college and/or work readiness.

Chapter 7

High School Juniors & Seniors: Ready, Set? Not Quite Yet

Are you college or workforce ready?

Lights, camera, GRADUATION! Have a general idea or plan for what happens after high school graduation: attend college, learn a trade, enroll in a branch of the armed services, or learn business skills for school-to work opportunities.

So now college is around the corner and parents are biting their nails trying to figure out the right path to take. Most parents want their children to be "successful little versions" of themselves or to continue the family tradition generation after generation. In respect for their parents and grandparents, they trudge off to college with deep regrets regarding this decision and endure their "four year" time until graduation. The acquired degree produces yet another "doctor, lawyer or nurse" just like dad and grandpa and great-great grandpa, too.

In reality parents should simply ask the child what he or she would like to be and then figure out how mom and dad can help get them there without going bankrupt to pay college tuition. They might just surprise you with a few ideas of their own! Today's choices for a fulfilling career are far more creative then what we imagined. Social media, forensic science/DNA, robotics, plastic surgeons, pharmaceuticals, entrepreneurship, athletic trainers, radiology, and many more careers await the eager high school graduate who is willing to explore and find resources to reach their final destination.

But what about the student who *does not* want to be a life-long learner and has decided not to pursue further education after high school? For parents, their college dreams have been interrupted by a blaring important message that must be addressed. Remember, it's supposed to be the "student" who makes the ultimate decision for their future career and the following options could be a few options for consideration:

Armed Services

Here are 5 reconstructed branches of Military in United States with its own specific mission:

Branch of Service	Service Mission
ARMY—this is the largest and oldest	Acts as main ground force of the United States with a 4-Star General or Army Chief of Staff in command
AIR FORCE—fighter aircraft makes up tankers, light/heavy bombers, transports and helicopters	Defends the United States through air and space with Airforce Chief of Staff in command
NAVY—called on to work with many of the armed services branches	Maintains freedom of the seas with 4-star Admiral or Chief of Naval Operations in command
MARINE CORPS—responsible for the assaults, captures and control for enemy attacks	Executes actions by land, sea and air operations with a 4-star General and Commandant of the Marine Corps

<table>
<tr><td>COAST GUARD—this is the smallest and youngest</td><td>Conducts variety of tasks by boat, ship, aircraft and shore stations with 4-star Admiral or Coast Guard Commandant</td></tr>
</table>

Most people want to know which branch is the hardest to join, but in reality they are all psychological and emotional aspects of the physical 6-week basic training. Research their history and suggestions for which branch of service matches up to the type of career and rank that fits you best since they are all important in protecting the United States. Weigh the pros and cons of each one and visit their local branch offices for more information regarding qualifications, pay, benefits, retirement and active duty requirements.

Before you line up to join, everyone must pass many tests before wearing a uniform to defend on our United States' soil. The Armed Forces Qualifying Test (AFQT) is a subset of the Armed Forces Vocational Aptitude Battery (ASVAB) and each branch has its own. The test is broken down in to several categories including:

- Word knowledge (word definitions)

- Paragraph Comprehension (read more!)

- Mathematics Knowledge (concepts)

- Arithmetic Reasoning (word problems)

- Career Choice (based on ASVAB score)

If you are a little rusty from high school, brushing up on basic math, reading and writing skills will help with passing this exam. Take practice tests. Decide on a career. Hundreds of recruits are doing the same thing. The military is serious business and passing this test will determine if you are a good fit for the branch in which you have chosen. Here are required scores if you have already earned a high school diploma:

Airforce	Score: 36	If GED, need 65
Army	Score: 31	If GED, need 50
Coast Guard	Score: 40	If GED, need 50
Marine Corps	Score: 32	If GED, need 50
Navy	Score: 35	If GED, need 50

Trade Schools

If you want the fastest route to a job without taking college courses, then attending a trade school or vocational school is one route to go. So who wins the workforce race: the tortoise or the hare? Well, let's see. If school is not your passion, then getting a high school diploma or certificate from a public or private trade school will get you in the employer's door faster than going to school for two or four years. They offer hands-on experience and you can enter directly into the workforce in a specified field like plumbing, electric, cosmetology, Heating Ventilation and Air Conditioning (HVAC), etc. and take home a really high base salary to boot.

However, if you find that going back to school to get an associate's degree will enhance your salary and offer stability in the workforce even more, then I guess the tortoise wins this one. You'll have to stick it out for two years. The good news? Many employers now pay the cost of the tuition as an incentive to stay. Whether you are the tortoise or the hare, being debt-free of college loans is a win/win for all.

School-to-Work Programs

If you are a high school student, school-to-work programs are a great way to build quality resumes and gain comparable work experience. For seniors, this approach is the most dynamic because they can develop real-life work experience in their field of choice to see if it's the right career fit. These programs teach work responsibility, co-worker collaboration, leadership skills and professional development strategies to sustain employment. School programs also help build resume experience, teach supervisory expectations, understand employee roles and learn skills to apply for job positions that match personality and career applications.

Two-Year Community College

Don't let local community colleges fool you. Their course study associate degree programs can be just as rigorous as a university or accredited 4-year college. It takes time, commitment and strong work ethics to go to school and take care of a family. Since the community college competes with universities and other private colleges around them, they must offer competitive majors and degree programs to reach more diverse students. Maintaining a high

Grade Point Average (GPA) is critical especially if a student transfers to a 4-year institution to finish a bachelors and masters degree program of their choice.

Some associate degrees offer a base salary of $45-60K per year which is just as compatible as a 4-year degree to start. Community Colleges are offering so much more in continuing education in other areas, too such as professional development, personal enrichment and technical education to reach the community workforce.

Entrepreneurship

Owning your own business is based on commitment, excellent customer service, market research, management and financial risks. So why take on such burden and responsibility when there is a possibility of the business' failure? Well, the flip side is to keep working 40-50 hours a week for a company or corporation or work for yourself and earn a reputation for a good quality product or service to the community. Here are some obstacles that might come into play while being an entrepreneur:

- Reaching the right target market

- Making a product or service better than your competitor's

- Keeping up with technology

- Finding the right location or space to reach selected market

- Sustaining the business

- Managing employees

- Maintaining financial records and filing taxes

Some small businesses operate out of their home or virtual office if they cannot afford to lease an office space. Networking with other business owners is the key to staying in business and maintaining sustainability and growth. Some business owners believe that if you are not "networking," you are not working. Everyday should be an opportunity to sell your business services and attract the next client.

Certificate Programs

These programs are often offered by universities and community colleges to students who would rather bypass taking college courses and earning a degree. They are also less expensive and take less time to acquire unlike a degreed program which can take as long as two to four years. Most certificate programs fall into the following categories:

- Healthcare
- Paraeducator
- Early Childhood Education
- Bartending
- Bookkeeper
- Food Preparation
- English as a Second Language
- Baby Sitting
- Computer Technology
- Social Media
- Personal Trainer
- Security Guard
- Graphic Design
- Manufacturing
- Automation Technology
- Wedding and Event Planner
- Welding

Depending on the college or university size, there are even more certificate programs are being offered to serve the community's needs for certain employment workforce demands.

Internships

Whether paid or unpaid, **internships** are perfect for students who are looking to fulfill their professional practice with the experience of being in a real-world company or business under the supervision of management. Some internships can last six weeks to six months pending on the type of professional field. Some types of internships may include:

- Work studies

- Ambassadors

- Volunteer trainees

On the other hand, **apprenticeships** offer full time employment while learning business skills during the practice experience. This is more serious since wages are attached and after the apprenticeship is over, the student can move up within the company now that experience has been acquired and applied in real-world situations. These programs also pay a lot more than internships since more responsibilities are attached to the wage earned. Both programs enhance a student's resume and opens doors for even greater career opportunities in their chosen field of practice.

Still can't decide? Here are a few more areas of careers to consider:

- Accounting/Finance
- Architect
- Advertising
- Anthropology
- Arts & Entertainment
- Auto
- Book Author
- Business
- Caregiver
- Clergy
- College Adjunct
- Computer Technology
- Construction
- Cosmetology
- Delivery Driver
- Education
- Engineering
- Entertainment
- Entrepreneurship
- Executive
- Exercise/Movement Therapy
- Financial Services
- Fireman
- Forensics
- Government
- Healthcare
- Hospice
- Hospitality
- Human Resources
- Insurance
- Janitorial
- Journalism
- Law
- Legal
- Medical
- Mental Health
- Modeling
- Mortuary Science
- Motivational Speaker
- Music
- Nannies
- News Anchor/Reporter
- Non-Profits
- Phlebotomist
- Photographer
- Physical Therapist

- Physician/Physician's Assistant
- Policing
- Politics
- Professor (College)
- Radio
- Real Estate
- Repair/Remodeling
- Retail
- Sales
- Science
- Seamstress/Tailor
- Singer
- Sitters (Baby or Pet)
- Speech Therapist
- Sports (Athlete, Commentator or Coach)
- Technology
- Transportation
- Travel/Tourism
- Urban Planning
- Video Gamer
- Waiter/Waitress
- Wedding/Event Planner
- Workshop Trainer
- Writer

I know we've just scratched the surface in finding a career, but at least there are many choices for consideration. Many high school guidance counselors encourage students to take career surveys and tests to discover job skill matches or even pursue interest in various careers. This way, the foundation is laid for the right degree rather than being an undeclared major in college.

Spending additional money on classes you may not need or finding out that you have a weak stomach or faint at the sight of blood is something that is important if you have started a nursing career as a hospital neo-natal nurse in the maternity department. What's really important is strategically pursuing a career with longevity that will not become obsolete in 5-10 years but show promising areas of growth with opportunities to move up the ladder as workforce trends continue to change.

Graduation in Formation

Here's a reconstructed high school graduation check list. Most students get a part-time job just to keep up with the graduation dues, fees and costs to make this a memorable life event. Here's a peek at a reconstructed graduation packet check list:

Year book	$140.00	Check ordering deadline dates
Senior Pictures	$210.00	Make-Ups $225.00
Senior Ring	$300.00	Check ordering deadline dates
Cap & Gown	$56.00	Must attend 3 Practices
Senior Trip	$513.00	Half Deposit needed to hold seat
Prom	$75.00	No entry without ticket
Textbook Return	$145.00	Paid Receipt to Advisor
Scholarship Reference Letters & Scholarships		At least 3 written letters from teachers, coaches or mentors; At least 10 scholarship applications completed with attached essays
Lunch Account Balance		Paid Receipt to Advisor
Library Book Return		Confirmation to Librarian; save receipt

Fees, Cap and Gown

You can't walk with your high school class if you have outstanding library fees or overdue books, unreturned textbooks, cafeteria lunch balances or haven't ordered and paid for your cap and gown by the graduation practice date.

Guidance counselors are aware of these outstanding debts and may have already met with their selected group of student offenders. For example, Mrs. Smith has students with last names of A-D and Mr. Doe has students E-H, etc. Larger high schools with more than 1,500 students can be more difficult to meet with seniors pending on the counselor/student number ratio, especially if they are short staffed.

Pictures, Please: Say Cheese And Class Rings with "Class"

Not only are senior pictures expensive, but it's not the traditional graduation picture that we are used to making fun of back in the day. Now pictures are shown with backgrounds of parks, waterfalls, nature trails, and animals if you want it but the untraditional thing is this: they get to wear street clothes! Of course everyone looks alike in the school yearbook but the picture sent to Granny Agnes is just not the same. Even the rings are non-traditional. You name the design, it's in the catalog. Rings can cost up to $500 pending on the number of diamonds and gold setting. Josten's is still the top pick in class rings since 1897 and always will be. If it's not Josten's then it's just not a class ring.

Year Book: One Last Look

If you couldn't afford senior pictures or your class ring, then hold on to your seat for the good times and memories in the class yearbook. Yearbooks can range from $25-$250 pending on the custom features, upgrades, paper quality, and hand-sewn hardcover binding. More yearbook pages, the higher the price. Fewer yearbook pages, the lower the price. Don't forget to get your classmates to sign it. That way when the 25-year reunion rolls around, you'll be able to put the "MVP in Football," "Prettiest Cheerleader" and "Most Popular" faces with the *"Gosh, you haven't changed a bit"* names from the *"Glad you signed my yearbook"* so that I know who you really were back then. Um, I still don't recognize the "Homecoming King & Queen" at this reunion. Could they please stand up? Ok, you can sit back down, now. Yikes!

Prom Promise--This is Last One

Ok, this is the granddaddy of them all.

Young Ladies' Check List:

- prom gown
- Cinderella glass slippers
- diamond tiara
- matching jewelry
- limousine service
- pedicure

- manicure
- massage
- hair salon
- pre-party photo shoot
- professional party photo shoot at prom
- after-party photo shoot
- hotel room stay with BFF
- party favors, cake, balloons and gifts
- all-night room service
- morning breakfast
- final photo shoot

Young Men's Check List:

- $50 rented tuxedo at nearest mom and pop formal rental shop
- corsage
- hair cut
- Polaroid keep sake picture
- return tuxedo before rental shop closes

For some parents, this is like a junior wedding coupled with miniature brides and grooms. Some parents have confessed going well over their budget and spending over $2,000 on prom. Students are happy to report all their parents' finances from the prom dress (almost $500) and the rest was simply to compliment the "one-time" special occasion. The after-prom party is a separate expense altogether and I won't mention the food and beverage menu at the hotel with blocked reserved rooms and adult chaperones. Between the DJ and the decorations, it was truly a junior wedding with stressed out chaperone moms gliding around the hotel knocking on reserved room doors in their soft fuzzy slippers until 4 a.m.

Graduation Practice & Dress Code

It's just like being at work: if you are late, you get docked. If you are not at graduation practice, your diploma will be mailed to the address on file.

Graduation practices are very serious in nature and require full attention, participation and following precise instructions. For schools with 300 or more graduates, it can take a few hours to run through and sometimes the practices may relocate off school grounds in such facilities as a stadium, college campus gymnasium, or other modified location. Caps and gowns are expected to be purchased before hand and sometimes worn during practice to work through garment mishaps and malfunctions. Students who don't follow directions or take practice seriously are usually escorted out or gently reprimanded. For seniors heading to first-year college, this is great practice for business casual dress.

Males traditionally wear dress black pants, white collared shirts, black dress shoes and tie color matched with school colors. Females are expected to wear white dresses and white shoes. As a rule, high heeled shoes over 3 inches are not preferred since one could trip or overturn an ankle which is why low-heels or flats are encouraged on graduation day for safety measures.

Senior Trip

This usually depends on whether the school is going international or staying within the United States. The price also depends on the length of stay, means of travel (bus or airplane), and itinerary excursions. Most often the school staff accompanies the senior trip as chaperones and student waivers are signed by parents. This trip also seals in memories of their high school career and will be remembered for years to come.

College Trunk Party

By now, parents are financially tapped out and drained from all the high school activities that required yet another swipe or chip insert of their Master or Visa credit card. Since college starts in the fall, summer is spent packing and buying supplies for the ultimate dormitory experience. Trunk parties have become the social trend since family, relatives and friends can contribute to the supplies list while the parents can financially take a financial breather. In reality, this is the official end of their son or daughter's high school career and parents can proudly tap the good seal stamp on their foreheads: "RESPONSIBLE ADULT." Sure, they will still call home asking for more money and sharing their college problems, situations and decisions, but your gentle nudges and sweetie pie whispers of *"remember to get a job on campus"* during the trunk party will eventually pay off.

GED or High School Diploma?

So this chapter has talked about the big SENIOR year and choosing a career after high school graduation. But what about the students who dropped out and are now competing in the workforce without a high school diploma? Talk to anyone who has dropped out of high school and they will tell you that they wish they had that diploma in their hands right now! There are people just like you and me who had certain circumstances that prevented them from finishing high school which may include the following:

- Unplanned pregnancy

- Found job to support family or parents

- Became caregiver to parent or guardian

- Moved around a lot from parent being in military service

- Not interested in school

- Joined armed forces from draft or went to war

- Left home for personal reasons

- Repeated truancy at school

- Major or severe illness

- Learning Disabilities

- Got married in high school

There are two ways to get a diploma: through a GED (General Education Diploma) certificate program or attend night school at a local James H. Groves Adult High School. The difference is that the Adult High School helps students earn the diploma in a few years and includes all subjects, courses, electives and credit simulation of being at an accredited school. For students who just need a few credits, credit recovery courses are also available and can make graduation a reality.

On the other hand, the GED crams four years of schooling into 40-60 hours (per month) of studying and reviewing over the course in 6-12 months pending on student class availability and time invested in GED online and study programs. Subjects reviewed include the following:

- Reading Language Arts and Written Essay

- Math

- Social Studies

- Science

So think of it this way: instead of delving deeply into the historical eras for a full semester in *social studies*, students get a brief snapshot and introduction of what really happened at the Boston Tea Party, The Emancipation Proclamation, Pearl Harbor, World War I & II, and other major important turning points in history. In *math*, basic concepts are reviewed including algebraic expressions, fractions, integers, decimals, reading charts and graphs and word problems, etc. Since *science* also introduces mathematical similarities, students get an overview of basics including earth and space, biology, chemistry and physics. In *reading language arts*, basic concepts include reading strategies, skimming and scanning, comprehension, main ideas, complex analysis, compare and contrast, responding to text, vocabulary, spelling, grammar and mechanics and usage.

In passing the GED test, most students combine math and science study strategies to build learning strategies in math reasoning and practice.

Similarly, reading and writing is also combined since the learning strategies go hand-in-hand with mastering the required concept skill sets. In the classroom, students are supported with tutors, academic support, practice drills and can take a Pre-GED test to see if they are ready. Here's an overview of passing scores to earn the certificate:

• MTH	(Math)	145+
• SCI	(Science)	145+
• RLA	(Reading Language Arts & Writing)	145+
• SST	(Social Studies)	145+

When it comes to the GED or the High School Diploma, employers differ in which is the best. Some say they want the original diploma and that the GED holds no weight in contrast. It also depends on the organization, company or college who determines your fate. Most people are hired without a diploma and then somewhere down the line, the employer requires this document to continue employment. This is tough especially if a person has been working without it over the last 10, 20 or 30 years.

Most students enrolled in a day or night GED program may have dropped out due to a situation beyond their control and could not return to school despite their circumstances at the time. The hardest part for most is trying to go back and finish but even five, 10, 20 and 30 years later, life events (including unemployment) still continue to be the main barrier to enroll and earn their GED in a selected day or night programs.

Did you know that.....

...some student loan borrowers do not pay back their debt resulting in wage garnishments and IRS tax refunds intercepted for immediate repayment?

...student loan debt is second largest debt with home mortgage being number one?

...most students are not interested in reading e-books or any books in hard or soft cover?

...many students do not know how to navigate through the sections (A, B, C, D, E, etc.) of a local newspaper?

...most high school students are unable to orally communicate or write on their grade level?

...Toastmasters clubs offer strategies and workshops on public speaking and are located throughout the United States?

...85% of college students procrastinate when turning in course work assignments?

...some employers and colleges do not consider the GED certificate <u>equivalent</u> to a High School Diploma?

WORD of the Day: IDEALOGY—study of ideas throughout society: socially, politically, historically and literary

Your Turn Activity:

1. **What are the 5 branches of military service?** List oldest branch first:

      ____

      ____

      ____

      ____

      ____

Which branch would you select and why? (See Page 126 to review)

____

____

____

____

____

2. **Name 4 core subjects and 4 electives required to graduate high school:**

Subjects	Electives

3. **Name at least 3 career choices: (See Page 131-132)**

Where do you see yourself three years from now? Five years from now? What if your career becomes obsolete? What are your next steps to get back in the workforce?

____

____

____

Chapter 7 Notes

Chapter 7 Notes

CHAPTER 8

Step 8: Learn to speak and write fluently to a general audience.

Chapter 8

13 powerful Words: Improving vocabulary

Does your vocabulary match your grade level?

If you can't express yourself orally or in written form, reading more is the cure. Knowing more vocabulary also helps with comprehension on quizzes, tests, and exams.

Be authentic in your word choice and vocabulary: written communication. I received this as a keepsake from my aunt a few years ago. It was a copy of my mother's homework project assignment in "Vocational Home Economics" back in 1951 at her high school in Maryland.

3

HOME PROJECT A

PLAN OF WORK FOR YOUR HOME PROJECT

1. What is the title of your Home Project?   (See pages 1 and 2)
2. Why have you chosen this Home Project? How will it be useful to your family?
3. Plan and do your reference reading before you start your project. Record on page 5. Record also the reference reading you do during the projects and any helps received from any source.
4. Outline the definite tasks to be done. These should be placed in the order in which you plan to do them.
5. Plan for the number of weeks probably required to finish your Home Project. On what days of the week do you plan to work on your Project?
6. Insert extra paper for illustrations, drawings, samples of materials, or recipes.

The name of my project is "Preparing Desserts Over Week-Ends."

The reason I choose this project is to become more familiar with cooking and preparing desserts.

Here's an original copy of her History Report. I am still amazed at her remarkable penmanship and vocabulary back then. She cursive wrote a 6-page paper and received a B+. (I'm guessing her teacher took off points because her blue pen ran out of ink and she wrote the rest of the paper in black ink.)

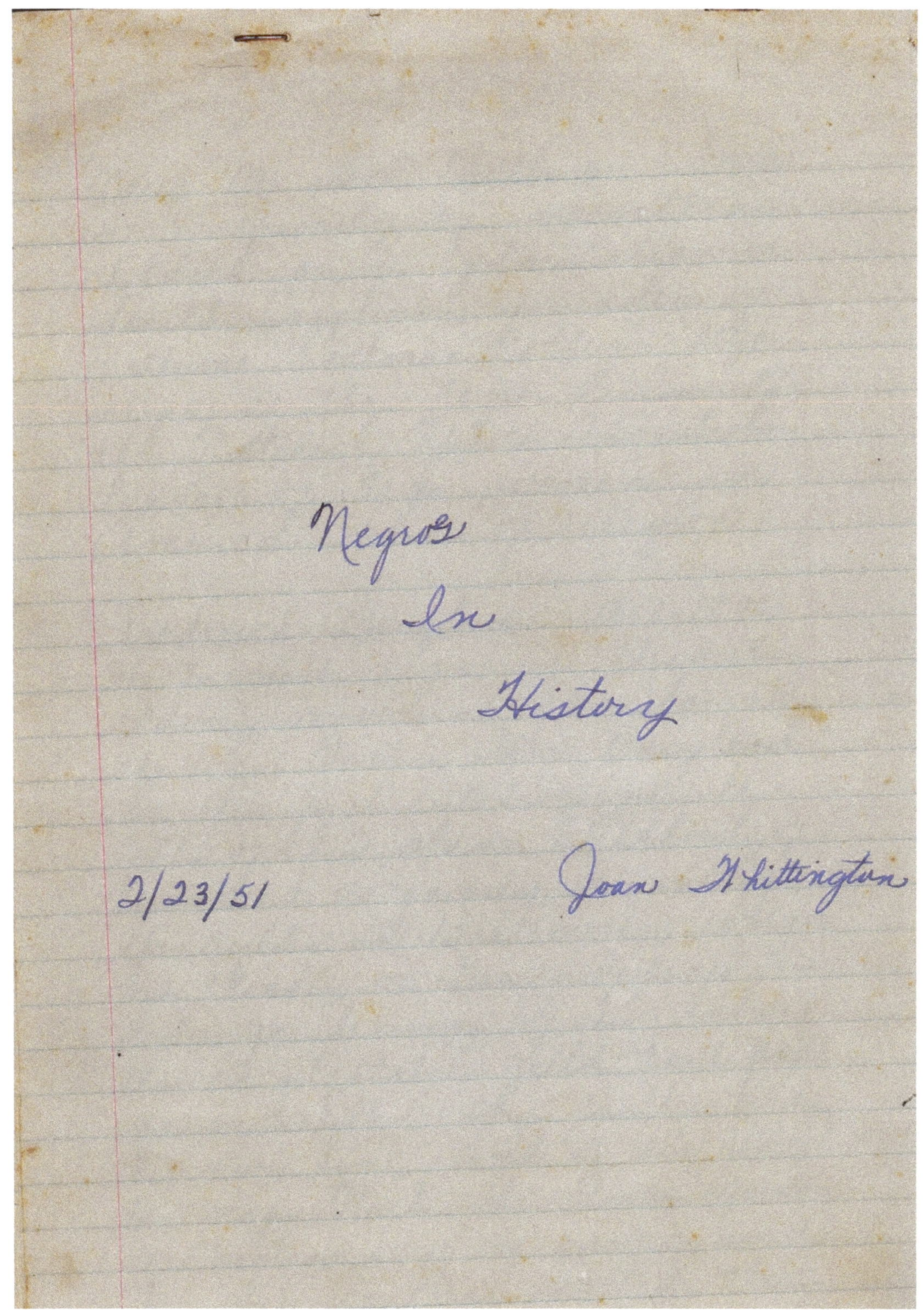

* <u>Mary Mc Leod Bethune</u>: born
in a family of seventeen
children on a plantation in
South Carolina; founder of
Bethune Cookman College; organizer of the Negro-division of
the National Youth Admistration;
leader of Negro-women in
America. Lover of religion.

* <u>Frederick Douglass</u>: (1817-1875)
The foremost negro in the anti-
slavery movement, was born. A
slave in Eastern Shore Maryland.
In his first autobiograph he
tells of his slave childhood, of
his work as family servant for
the aulds in Baltimore; where
his kindly mistress awakened his
desire for learning; of his labor
as a plantation field hand and
as a skilled ship caulker hiring
his own time, and of his attempt
to escape North. The slavery experience
of Douglass were so varied, and
he was so clear sighted, that

his autobiographies give one of the most convincing and deeply moving feeling. His first book was "Narrative of the Life of Frederick Douglass" (1845) "My Bondage And My Freedom" "Life and Time of Frederick Douglass" Douglass was a slave, transformed into a statesman and leader. He was a defender and defended, the voice and symbol of what Negro might become.

III.

W. E. B. Du Bois: born in a New England village just after the Civil War, educated at Harvard And Berlin, brilliant writer of Classic English; elder statesman of his race. He has been a great worker in the N. A. A. C. P. and founder of the "Crisis" magazine.

William Edward Burghardt Du Bois born February 23, 1868. He has many great Contributions for his race.

4. <u>Walter White</u>:
Secretary of the N. A. A. C. P.
organization. He is a leading
crusader for civil rights for all
people. He was born in Atlanta
on July 1st, 1893. Author of novels,
essays, and has received the
Spingian Medal award.

5.
<u>Ralph Bunche</u>: was born in
Detroit and educated at the
University of California and Howard.
He is a world-leader and plays
an important role in the United
Nations organization. He is head
of the Department of <u>Political</u>
<u>Science</u> at Howard University
but is now on leave for ten
years. The Author of many books
and articles.

VI. Caldendar of Events:

Negroes In History:

1. A. Philip Randolph

2. George Washington Carver

3. Modecar H. Johnson

4. Paul Robeson

5. Langston Hughes

6. Garter G. Woodson

7. Richard Wright

8. Haile Selasie

9. James Weldon Johnson

10. Booker T. Washington

11. Charles S. Johnson

12. Alain Locke

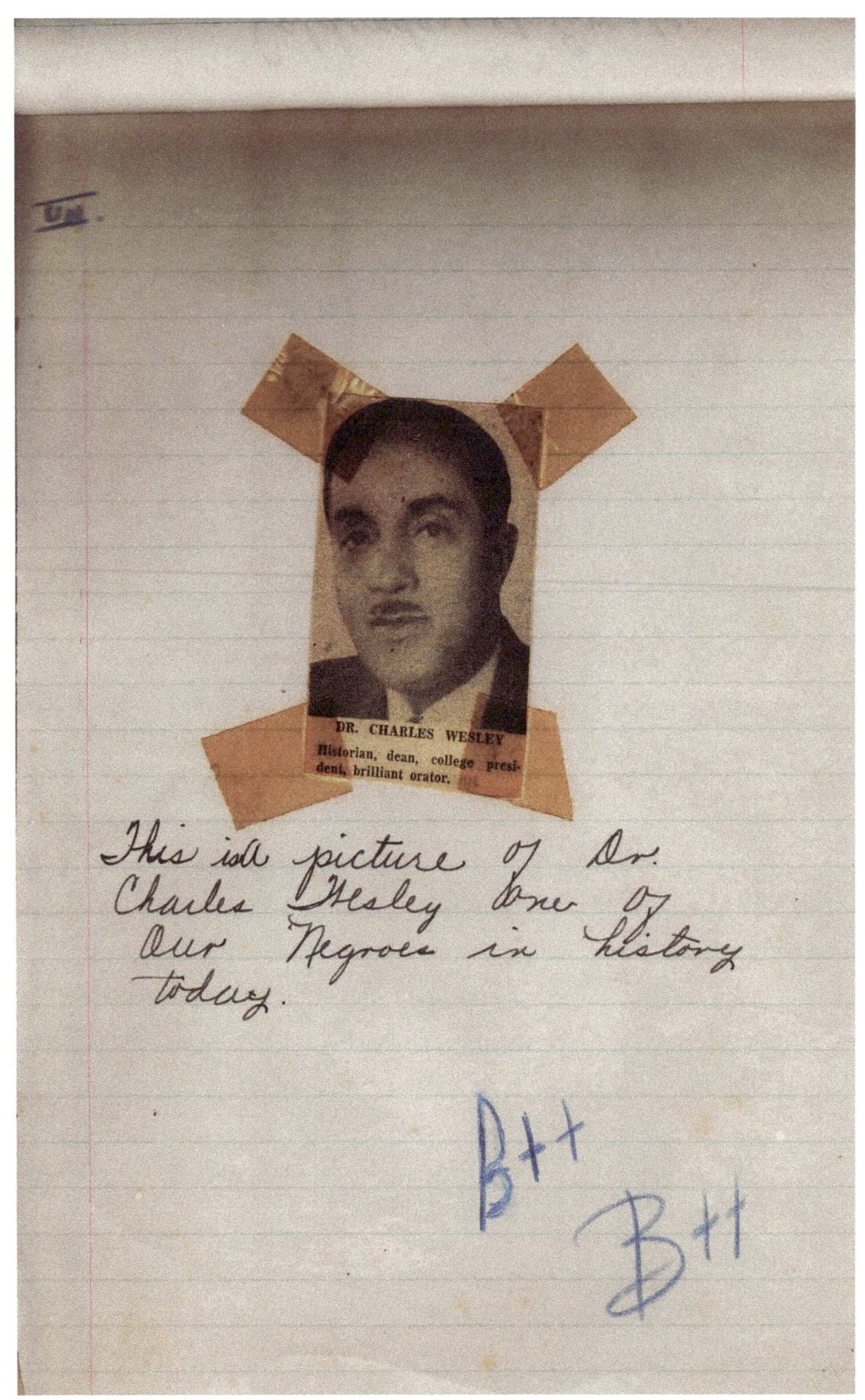

This is a picture of Dr. Charles Wesley one of our Negroes in history today.

B++

B++

Be Authentic in Your Word Choice and Vocabulary: Verbal Communication in Our Nation

Now let's forward to the early 1980's for another form of communication: oral. We could stop to ask anyone for directions and in return they would rapidly wave their arms and point fingers in awkward directions trying to explain how to get you on Interstate-59. *What kind of vocabulary was being used back then?* Plenty of verbs: turn, stop, look, slow down, go past the third house, etc.

Fast forward to 2019 and after several miles of *Driving Miss Daisy* in the slow lane, people pass by giving obscene finger gestures as you squint to find exit signs for the mystery Orange Route. *What kind of vocabulary is being used now?* Frustrated, you stop *again* at a gas station to get more directions, more finger pointing and flailing arms only to end up somewhere in Montana now headed to the Apple Hill Mall. Back then, we used the Rand McNally Atlas Map (nearly two feet tall when unfolded) sprawled out on the front seat. Now with GPS (Global Positioning System) in our car with computer voices that keep us company until we reach our destinations and maps on our cell phones, no wonder people struggle with basic communication skills. The hard work is being communicated through the GPS system or car radio speaker in a broad array of words, traffic signals, vivid directions, loud beeps and tinkling bells. It even tells you how fast you are speeding, the nearest rest stop and upcoming traffic lights with cameras to warn you of running a red light. Funny thing is that even modern technology still gets you lost and driving in circles trying to find the final destination arrow on the GPS that keeps *recalculating…..*

In our fast paced world, **vocabulary** is an important tool and still requires "real people" to communicate information to others, especially on standardized tests. But most commonly, communication is very critical in the workplace since this is where most people spend 5-8 hours a day, 5-7 days a week. For example, your supervisor asks you to put together a presentation for the district directors at next Friday's meeting and sweetly adds, "*By the way, can you make the presentation at least an hour? Order lunch, too, and I'll reimburse so save your receipt.*" A pat on the back and song whistling follows as your boss happily tips out for a 2-hour lunch and won't be back until next Tuesday. So that you don't wet your pants and get in the Walgreen's line for the Poise Pads on sale for *big leaks,* here are 12 Powerful Words you need to know in order to communicate with your peers **before** that important District Meeting:

1. Summarize It:
Just Put it in your Own Words

Teachers are famous for saying, "Make sure you put this in your own words *when you write the summary.*" Notice the teacher specifically did not say "*when you cut and paste it from the article you found on the internet.*" **A summary just tells the main idea or basic concept in simple terms** and in your own words. For example, give a quick summary of the last movie you saw, not the details.

If you watch NetFlix, Tubi, or Roku, short summaries of movies and shows are given in one or two sentences to help you get an overview of what to watch or not simply based on the summary. Almost everything can be summarized to give a general understanding of the overall gist. In the workplace, keeping the general idea simple saves a lot of time, helps with getting buy-in from other departments, and makes it easier to collaborate when achieving mission goals. Here are some basic summary examples:

- course or class offered (syllabus overview)

- novel (back cover preview)

- play (playbill)

- sermon (place for notes on church bulletin)

- lecture (brochure summary)

- handbook (overview for specific audience)

2. Explain It:
Tell the Short Version, Not the Details

Explaining can get tricky. Ask a 5 year-old to explain how Santa gets down their chimney every year to deliver Christmas presents and this could take a while. But in simple terms, **explaining just means to include these simple 5 W's** or categories that can pretty much tell the whole story without extra verbiage (the long, drawn out details). Just keep it simple:

- **Who**—usually a person, group, organization, family, celebrity, etc.

- **What**—primary focus, key point

- **Where**—the place, setting or location; can be a city, state, nation, country or specific region

- **W**hen—recent, last month, last year or decades ago; give specific calendar date (dd, mm, year)

- **W**hy—matters to the general public, certain culture gender, race, religion or population

- (Sometimes **H**ow)—how it happened or came about

3. Support It:
The Back-Up That Stays With You

When Tidy Tim (an untidy bully) kept taking my lunch money in elementary school, it felt good to have my brother make him give it back. That's what good about support. *It simply means that the main idea needs back up details from the story.* This proves that you know what the story is about and the details back up what you say. For example, if the story talks about why milk is good for you then you locate the facts that shows such proof: like research, statistics, proven techniques, updated technology or results from studies found directly in the story or article.

4. Describe It:
Tell a Tall Tale (Not too Tall)

Story telling is popular with small children because the more vivid the picture the better the story. Since the picture shows the action, descriptive words have to work even harder to bring the story to life when reading out loud. Now we can picture *The Three Bears* coming home to an upset house while Goldilocks has no respect for other people's property and sleeps in their beds. Now picture the poor *Three Little Pigs* constantly running from house to house while the big, bad wolf keeps blowing them all down after such effort to keep rebuilding new ones. The wolf doesn't care about the insurance policies the three pigs have filed or how high their policies are now that they are considered high risk homeowners! So in simple terms, descriptive words consist of these 5 words:

Seeing, tasting, touching, hearing and smelling. In the descriptions below, there's no inkling of visualization in these examples:

- we "smelled" the biscuits in the oven

- she "heard" the car stop outside

* they "tasted" the s'mores

* we "saw" the sunset

* I "felt" my hand burning

In order to actually describe something, **you should be able to visualize it in your mind.** Now let's try using the same 5 senses to bring more life into the above examples.

* The buttery aroma of the homemade sweet potato biscuits made our mouths water!

* The red sports car came to a screeching halt on the black diamond asphalt.

* We savored the yummy, chocolate gooey marshmallow s'mores over the fire pit.

* The sunset was breathtaking and heavenly in coral red and plum purple.

* I screamed in pain when my finger singed and burned on the hot stove!

Now we can actually **visualize** what just happened. Can't you just taste those piping hot, buttery biscuits melting in your mouth? The sports car didn't just stop, but it actually screeched shrill enough to put hands over their ears when it finally stopped. Whenever you see a beautiful sunset, it just takes your breath away beyond description. And that's the way visualization works. If you can picture it in your mind, then you've done an excellent job putting it into words.

5. Formulate It:
Make a Systemized Plan

To **formulate** means to *come up with a systemized plan to prepare or do something for a specific purpose.* A perfect example is when students have to come up with a science project and have one week to complete it. A systemized plan might look something like this:

Monday
* Decide brochure or Power Point Presentation
* Review project requirements
* See examples for ideas
* See teacher for clarifications, rubric and expectations

Tuesday

- Draft or sketch main ideas for project requirement
- Select graphics, fonts, sub-heads and title
- Find quiet room to work and be creative

Wednesday

- Lay out slides or brochure's 6 sides (front/back cover, etc.)
- Match pictures, use color graphics and titles for each section
- Make information flow; hook the reader

Thursday

- Type all copy for professional look; do not handwrite on brochure
- Proofread for spelling and grammatical errors
- Practice presentation orally for time required (follow rubric guidelines)
- Keep project in safe place away from pets or small children

Friday

- Dress professionally—it shows the effort put into your work
- Arrive early to prepare and review presentation
- Be the first to present—use expression, excitement and involve audience
- Follow highest rubric score to ensure best possible grade

6. Synthesize It: Change Along the Way

This is not the musical instrument synthesizer, but another writing term used in the classroom starting at the middle school level through college. When readers read, sometimes a story can change their perception as they think through the *exposition* (beginning problem) and the series of events that lead to the *resolution* (solving problem). Pending on the story, along the way the reader develops an opinion followed by a well thought out conclusion.

For example, in the middle school book "*The Giver*" by Lois Lowry, 12-year-old Jonas lives in a utopian society that has taken away pain by giving everyone "sameness" but later discovers that it really is dystopian after all. He is chosen to be the next in line to inherit the daunting position of being the Receiver of Memory. Readers use synthesizing in this story and are challenged with this dystopian way of living versus their own value system and knowing good and evil based on the way parents raise their children.

7. Analyze It:
Break It Up and Think It Through

In literary analysis, students have to show how something is portrayed or used. For example, when an author uses personification to bring human qualities to an object, the teacher is looking to see if students understand **literary elements** in the story. Analyzing can be used in three ways to dig deeper:

- "think" it through—why would author use this particular example?

- "break the story up"—look at exposition and resolution; follow story clues

- break into even smaller pieces"—use questioning techniques to see all sides of author's point of view

When students analyze, they are reviewing and further developing critical thinking skills necessary for college preparation and in real-life situations. As they pass along the highways, church billboards can be a good example of how students could further analyze a **general idea** directed to the public. Let's proceed with caution as we analyze these reconstructed signs posted along the roadways. This one addresses summer vacation to school students:

God will <u>not</u> answer your repeated prayers about extending school vacations

Heaven is eternal; your summer vacation is not

Here's another reconstructed message for school teachers and instructors who might want a snow day off:

God might answer your prayers for snow days if everyone "touches and agrees" in snowfall degrees

I wondered if educators would interpret this message humorous or find it offensive. When students learn to analyze interpretations, it helps when they can understand the **general idea** and see the humor for which it was intended. If not, then the idea gets lost in the translation.

Here's a penny for your thoughts on this final reconstructed message for the general public (1) and church visitors (2) using an eternal guide check-up:

1. It's not all "downhill" unless you refuse to take the "uphill" road

2. Thought summer was a sizzler? Don't detour and go straight to "an all-seasonal" scorcher

Now this one is tricky because it requires critically thinking at its best. In literary elements, students will begin analyzing stories, articles, phrases, quotes, political cartoons, rhetoric and point of view perspectives written by the author covering all kinds of topics. In this case, religion can be the most subjective and will often bring about the most controversy in the classroom.

The good thing is that students will learn to use analysis to support their own ideas through personal experience and prior knowledge to support their opinions.

8. Evaluate It:
Rate It 5 Stars *****

We all do it. Evaluate the movie. Evaluate the instructor. Evaluate customer service. Evaluate the book. Evaluate the delivery service. It's what we do to let everyone know to either buy it or try it based on our opinion. We judge the worth of something by giving it a 5 star rate of quality:

Five	(5)	*****	(excellent)
Four	(4)	****	(very good)
Three	(3)	***	(good)
Two	(2)	**	(fair)
One	(1)	*	(poor)

It happens in math class, too when we are trying to find X or Y's *value* in the equation and come up with an answer that fits. Evaluate the school. Evaluate a new car. Evaluate your job performance. If you really think about this, evaluations are in every part of our lives. So the next time you see a movie rating of ½ star, it's a possibility that it really isn't worth the $9 you might pay for the ticket and you'll be glad you saved $20 on popcorn and a soda.

9. Infer It:
Read Between the Lines

Students learn how to **inference** through reading novels and getting to know the main character. However, if the protagonist is walking on the boardwalk along the beach wearing a heavy coat in the summer time, we can begin to infer three things:

- He/she has a medical condition

- He/she is mentally ill

- He/she is cold-natured

We just made an inference about what could be a logical reason for the character wearing a heavy coat in the summer heat. Inferencing helps students to *read between the lines* to get some possible answers about the coat, especially in 90 degree weather. Later in the novel, the author explains the reason for the heavy coat: the character suffered from a medical condition that initiated body chills from the medical prescription which produced bizarre physical side effects. Let's try another one:

In another story, an Englishman staggers to his car and crumbles to the ground holding his spinning head while sweating profusely. We can infer three things:

- He is a mere town drunk

- He has vertigo or a brain imbalance

- He is severely disabled and forgot his walker/cane

We've just made another inference about what could be a logical reason for the character staggering to his car. Later the author informs the reader that the man suffers from vertigo which gives the appearance of a drunken state when the brain is off balance. He was holding his head to stop it from spinning which later caused nausea and violent vomiting.

10. Predict It:
Make a Guess or an Assumption for the Sake of Argument

In reading literature, most students have to predict what will happen in the middle or at the end of story and answer questions. If the character has not resolved the problem by the end of the story, we now have to predict what will happen next. In "*The Necklace,*" by Guy de Maupassant no one could have ever guessed that the beautiful necklace worn just one night was made of paste or costume jewelry. When the necklace turns up missing, the characters go through great strife in repaying its owner a large sum of money over a period of time costing them years of unnecessary poverty, sickness and pain. Had the main character simply fessed up to her friend that she had lost the necklace in the first place, they would have laughed themselves silly at the mere thought of its true value. As a result, this assumption caused the main character a life of ruin in the end.

11. Trace It:
Do Not Pass Go and Collect $200 Just Yet

In short stories or novels, readers will have to go back in chapters to find information on major characters or events. To keep events in order, it helps to **annotate** (write down main ideas in phrases) along the margins to keep track of important dates, transitions, settings and various situations. For example, in "*The Poisonwood Bible*" by Barbara Kingsolver, it was important to keep track of the dramatic events told by the wife and four daughters of Minister Nathan Price who moves the family to the African Congo from the U.S. To many high school readers, this 500+ page novel is hard to follow, especially if they've never read the original King James Version (KJV) of the Bible and have to retrace events to understand the characters emotions, reasons for decisions, and painful events that transitioned their lives over the span of 30 years.

12. Identify It:
Reader vs. Character

Students are challenged more and more in literature and film to identify with characters in novels and movies. After the setting is established, identification begins through a psychological relationship between the reader and the author. Movies are more realistic since you can actually see the characters' performance on screen versus having to visualize the characteristics vividly described by the author in a novel. For example, when watching Alfred Hitchcock shows, psychotic characters become very clear and sinister motives can be simply observed in the setting: a shabby mansion, foggy graveyards, overgrown marshes, seedy characters, etc. On the other hand, Marvel Comics movie heroes like *Spiderman*, *The Hulk*, and *Aquaman* can be identified and related to in real life since the characters are often regular people who learn of their special powers to help save the world. An audience can ask themselves such questions as:

- How am I similar to this person before the heroic transition takes place?

- How is my personality different from the character?

- Do we have the same human qualities?

- Do we have the same mind set for bringing justice for all?

- If I were a super hero, would I want people to identify me in public?

In today's world of constant social media, it's becoming easier to relate with people who buy the latest technology, tote the most electronic devices, or have the most followers. But in order to stay different and original, it also becomes important to *identify with yourself* to stay creative, insightful and industrious to continue evolving into the best you that you can possibly be. Don't be fooled by getting caught up with "if everyone is doing it, it must be right so I'll jump on the bandwagon, too." Just because everyone is doing it, doesn't always make it right.

Did you Know that......

...most people rely on the internet or social media for all of their news and information?

...there are 4 types of vocabulary which includes listening, speaking, reading and writing?

...many students are not fluent or familiar with vocabulary they should already know to meet their grade level standards?

...reading fluently (books, magazines, newspapers, etc.) helps to improve sight word recognition and your daily vocabulary?

...over 5 billion searches are used on Google every day?

...senior citizens are <u>unlikely</u> to use the internet at all?

...most newspapers are written on a sixth grade reading level?

...many students have difficulty with spelling since weekly vocabulary lessons have been removed from elementary, middle and high schools?

WORD of the Day: TERMINOLOGY—vocabulary of specialized terms or words relating to a particular subject

Your Turn Activity:

1. **Explain to someone how to apply for a Library Card.** (Hint: they must go to a local library for the application form)

First….____

Then….____

Next…____

Finally…____

2. **Analyze the last movie you saw.** In your response, include the following information:

A. Time Period in movie vs. 2010. Name 3 things that were different 10 years ago
B. If movie was a remake, compare and contrast the original to the new version
C. What was the reason behind the movie title? Research your answer

3. **Evaluate the last class or course in which you or someone you know enrolled.** Use the 5 star evaluation to write about the experience in the lines given below:

   5= Excellent ____

   4= Very Good ____

   3= Good ____

   2= Fair ____

   1= Poor ____

In your opinion, how could the instructor improve the course? What other comments or suggestions do you have?

____

____

____

____

____

Chapter 8 Notes

Step 9: Understand that creativity, socialization and individual participation take place with "real people," not total dependence on television, computers, tablets, laptops, iPhones or other electronic devices in cyberspace.

Chapter 9

Research & Technology: *Using* Technical Etiquette

Alexa, can you write my 20-page research term paper?

Learn how to function without your cell phone or electronic device to be effective while participating in networking events, performing at the work place and attending professional business meetings.

There's nothing more inconvenient than being in a group that must produce a project in a matter of weeks. **Diversity** is a word that applies to all races, cultures and genders but unfortunately everyone has their version of right protocol and a perfect project. In order to function in a group, classroom, or job placement, we all must get along, cooperate with each other and most of all *respect one another's differences*.

In our imperfect world, sometimes we may face disrespect because of these differences which could be a reason why some people give up on their ideas and dreams: our unique co-workers make up a melting pot of memorable personality traits. We have to interact and collaborate with them on a projected outcome and the overall goal is that we all successfully meet the company's mission and department objectives.

Team Work Requires Working with Real People

In the real world, everyone has to work with co-workers from all walks of life. You'll find that working with a retiree can be a lot more stressful than working with a 17-year old high school student intern "who is technology savvy." Language barriers can also play a huge role when trying to communicate with someone who is just learning English as a Second Language. Sometimes disabilities, medical conditions, ignorance, and negative mindsets can lead to setbacks in working together to meet desired outcomes and initiatives for strong-willed employers who strive to make it on the "*Top 50 Best Employers to Work For.*" Employers want employees who stand out and go the extra mile in the work place. Let's look at reconstructed personality traits that are diverse and really could exist in the cubicle office near you:

People Pleasers

We all see them sitting quietly in the company cafeteria humming: very nice, well-mannered and well-liked people who are built to please but take leadership positions that sometimes might not really fit. Deficits such as inexperience, lack of self-confidence and self-doubt may cloud their judgement especially when it's time to make tough staff decisions which could lead to opposite personalities repeatedly taking advantage of them. Overall, they do a really good job and are always joyous around others.

Punch With Your Lunch

We accidentally bump into them not looking where we are going: strong-willed industrious leaders who might gently manipulate others in order to get what they want. Born with the ability to organize, their outstanding entrepreneurship skills can redevelop business strategies in a moment's notice. In the business world, they may come across somewhat bossy, a tiny bit insensitive to other's needs and will intimidate if necessary. If pushed, one could come face-to-face with a meaty fist if not in agreement with their philosophy. And just when you least expect it, there's a card and beautifully wrapped present on your desk at the year-end Christmas party.

Rockets Red Glare

You might not notice them at the department meeting: standoffish, a little arrogant, and very sheltered. If not noticed for their efforts, it might get a little red, white or blue ugly for patriotic sakes. When in disagreement, the red stare (or rocket's red glare) down comes out only near the water cooler and while waiting impatiently for the only staff bathroom. A blue temper just might flare when they find out there's no toilet paper or air freshener left from the last person who used it.

Lieutenant Columbos

They can blow smoke in white circles with a cigar, cigarette or vape pen: very grateful, good natured team players who just like coming to work and being a part of a wholesome initiative that helps the world and community as a whole. Very insightful and willing to help anyone from the president to the custodian. Clothes might be a little outdated but their sharp minds set office trends, especially in the field of technology, law, politics and leadership.

Water Cooler Pitchers & Switchers

They are the star in great mystery movies: scheming, pushy and persuasive. Often the outlier, they will get someone else to do all the work and wait for the kudos. Born crafty salespeople, they can sell anything and be the top sales guru of the week. There's no product that can't be sold! Everyone needs one if not now then next year. While hiding in back of the water cooler, an arm slips around your shoulders. How does this sound? You are overdue for having the newly remodeled staff lounge not only *named* after you, but they would be more than happy to write up a small contract to get paid making sure that it is spelled write, err right!

No Friend Zoners

The guitar and ukulele sits in special corner by their desk: usually musically or artistically talented, yet isolated in the workplace. Highly intelligent and knowledgeable about the world around them but friends are not a priority since they prefer to be alone. Work groups, parties and meetings are not the favorite. Often oblivious to others around them, communication is not a favorite, either unless the boss insists that this is for professional development. Ok, so it's not very professional. Just remember to knock on their imaginary "cubical" office door and don't touch their belongings without asking first—well, at least wash your hands, use sanitizer and put on rubber gloves, ok?

Sensitive Ones

Everyone wants to be a popular follower on social media: some followers need to confirm and reconfirm their followings with others. Very imaginative and creative but sometimes a little sensitive to criticism. Being able to hold something (coffee cup, files, supplies, etc.) serves as symbols of comfort and self-reassurance when in the presence of others. Often nice, caring people with neat appearance, fashionably color-coordinated and can spot a piece of lint on your shirt a mile away.

Complainers

Mother Nature could send a week of sunshine: perfect 75 degree days and a gorgeous clear blue sky but it's the wrong shade of blue and the sky needs more clouds but not too many. It's too cold or too hot. The color of the lunch room was a bad choice. People are hazards and nuisances, always in the way and everything is just an inconvenience. Anything you say will be challenged with a negative response and "I told you so." Clock in at 8 a.m. and complain until 4:30 p.m. It is believed that after a day acknowledging mistakes and faux pas among their co-workers, the company would surely go under without them on the payroll.

Knock, Knock Who's Where?

The life of a dull party: always with an infectious laugh and snort to boot. Enjoys having fun at any event, becomes friends with everyone and are delightful trendsetters in the workplace. When given a job, they go about it in fun ways that show their imagination through basic non-innovative ideas. Every week, homemade baked goods from granny's recipes are provided in the staff lounge for your enjoyment. Who doesn't like brownies with cream cheese smiley faces? Plus knock, knock jokes are only funny when they tell it in animated Sponge Bob voices.

Mustang Sallys

Time is well-spent on making <u>easy</u> decisions about <u>fun things:</u> holidays, birthdays, organizing parties and blowing up balloons. It doesn't require help or collaboration from others since important decisions spoil the party. Instead, it becomes chaotic when others get involved or offer an opinion that won't be fun to do. Just like math has a strategy for solving an algebraic equation, why do you think there is a major consultation with Aunt Sally first? We still memorize **P**lease **E**xcuse **M**y **D**ear **A**unt **S**ally. It helps to solve the equation in steps. First, start with numbers inside parentheses, then find the exponents, then multiplication followed by addition and finally subtraction. If a step is skipped, the whole problem ends up incorrect! For Aunt Sally, if *anyone* gets into this office equation, it ends up squashed, packed up, and U-Haul moved to the next building along with her new identity. Now. (Sally takes a deep breath and aligns 8 pencils on her desk) Then she sweetly asks, "Who in our department is having a birthday this week???? Yay!"

Know-It-Alls

How can one person know everything? Don't say a word because they already know: every conversation, phone call, emergency, board meeting and new employee. Plus, they are always right—and get defensive if challenged with true facts. Every answer is so long and drawn out that you can go to the bathroom, eat your lunch and the same conversation will still be going on long after you return. They know about you, your family, your wife's job, your neighbor's car, and reasons why your children shouldn't attend the private school across the street. Your job is only to listen. They know every football and basketball statistic, player contract salary amounts and they can rattle them off like credits at the end of a good movie. It's so annoying that one by one, the employee lunch room quickly empties out without them ever noticing.

Slugs

It's a super power to be able to sit all day pondering absolutely nothing: they won't cooperate, participate, generate or corroborate in anything that has to do with team work. They clock in, stay in the same position until quitting time and even then the chip on their shoulder says, "I hope I don't see you tomorrow." They know every payday and make sure their time sheets are in Human Resources first. There is no eye contact and morning greeting. No one can figure out how they got the job in the first place and made it through the interview process. Now comfortably tucked away in the corner of the department no one has even heard of, a brand new employee asks them for help. And a sort of pleasant reply without looking up from their i-Phone Combat 3000 is, "*That's not my job.*" After all, looking at a cell phone all day is really hard work.

Daydreamers

Make the best of every day: even if you see your co-worker floating by the window as you fill up your water bottle at the cafeteria water hole. Talking to them is like a dream and somehow everywhere you go, that dreamy fog follows you around sprinkling shiny magical glitter. Conversations are futuristic. E-mails are futuristic. Their dream jobs are futuristic. So what's real? Someday they will tell you but right now, the day dream lasts until the lunch break is over and then sadly they have to return back to their 1970's office grind.

Nosey Poseys

Some things are just plain private: your salary, who you date, where you live and how much you've saved for retirement. There's a difference between being concerned and just being nosey. They ask you 1,000 questions like a firing range and wait patiently for the answers while filing a chipped nail. When you read, they hover over your shoulder reading, too. They look in your desk, pick around in your recycling bin and always come in and linger even closer if you are on the phone and it sounds like a personal call. It never stops unless you call out from work and then they drop in on your co-worker next door to find out why you called out.

More ZZZZ's Pleeze

Every night is a party: last night, last weekend, and every Thursday, Friday and Saturday night. Getting through work is a chore since they haven't slept in weeks. Every conversation involves a plan to "catch up on sleep" but somehow it just never comes around. They doze off during meetings, use their lunch break for quick naps and close their office doors for a few more Z's. It just takes a mere mention of a get together after work and they spring back into a new party life without a "Z" and care in the world.

Amplified Sounds

You can hear them all the way down the hall: their volume voice is on loud at all times. If they are talking on the phone, everyone can hear the conversation. Everyone knows their family members by now because they have all called in at work. And when they laugh, it comes with a snort, hand clapping, feet stomping and ends with, "I know what you mean," at the end of every call. They are the sidebars who have to be hushed during meetings. They talk on their phones while in the bathroom and get louder when they flush. They play their cell phones on loud to hear the video, voice message or waiting for customer service. There is no off button or mute. When the phone rings, it plays the National Anthem really loud in pure HD amplified sound. Shhhhhh!

Messy Martians

They can tell you where everything is in their office: just give them a few minutes to find it. One look around and you can see the mounds of papers, piles of files, trash, old Chinese food plastic containers and the chopstick they couldn't find under your foot. The file cabinets are over stuffed, the computer is dusty and someone scribbled on the screen "*clean me*" and it coughs out loud by beeping every five seconds. The wardrobe is a little wrinkled but the person is a "genius at work" and often late to meetings. Don't worry, their excellent presentation skills will make you forget all about the time.

The Benevolent Ones

They carry a basket or push a cart: and it's always for a good cause. You need another job to keep up with the offering plate in this place. They peep in your office door and write your name down to give and if you don't, they will be back. No one ever knows where the money ends up. They just keep coming back for more. Your job? Just make it your business to get your name crossed off that chain letter list!

Time to Get to Work: Participation is Required

So now that you've met everyone at your dream job workplace, you heard or read somewhere in the employee handbook policy that participation would be required in the department as well as working with others to meet mission goals and improve quality assurance or something like that.

Thinking that this would never happen after your first 90 days, you start to get work e-mails like never before asking for your collaboration and expertise. At last, your participation is required.

RSVP ASAP

Ah! You've now settled into your comfortable office chair and the sweet aroma of hazelnut coffee and a fresh baked French cruller donut is ready to be savored. But somehow your breakfast fix is quickly interrupted when this red, white and blue e-mail pops up as "urgent" in your in-bin. It must be important because it's in the colors of the American flag and copied to all 500 employees in the department. There's no way to avoid it so it must be opened immediately and read very carefully:

Good morning, Staff!

Please mark your calendars and save the date for the next professional development meeting on the 15th. As discussed in the last meeting, you should begin working on your data contribution and design a Power Point to present to our executive board. Also attached is the new assignment for collaborative efforts with your new team along with the order of oral presentations.

Have fun with it! The rubrics are attached for time limits and data information must be included for each team. Should you have any questions, my hours are posted for availability.

Jane Doe

Director of Staff Development

After getting your thoughts together, you realize that your "participation is required" and procrastination is not an option. You hope for *Knock, Knock Who's Where* and *Lieutenant Columbo* teammates, but in reality you just might get *Punch With Lunch* and *Watercooler Pitch and Switch!* No matter who you end up with, you have to make it work to get the end result completed by the deadline date. It is also a reality that diverse personalities really do exist in your new workplace with a *Rocket's Red Glare* AND red bombs could really burst in air.

Creativity meets Originality

After you find out who your team is (take a deep breath here), a calm of relaxation should come over you along with a giant sigh of relief. No matter who is on your team, the end result must be creative and original. This requires some brainstorming on your behalf before that first initial meeting even takes place with the others. Employers like originality and creativity because it sets others apart from the norm. If you rely on Alexa for everything, you are already in trouble. If you rely on your children for everything, you are in even more trouble. If you rely on others for everything, then you will struggle with an unrealistic contribution of your own. Take the time to read the requirements of the team project and understand the rubric thoroughly. Now is the time to RUN not walk to Jane and tell her your concerns ahead of time so that you will not cause yourself added stress simply because you did not ask for clarity and guidance in the very beginning.

Socialization not Isolation

The office Christmas party is a must to attend. You can't hide in your office on December 22 forever and wish that your co-workers would go away. Aunt Sally will miss you and Amplified Sound will get on the loud speaker and call you out as a gentle courtesy. The ideas of socializing in the office place is a great way to know your co-workers since you spent more time with them throughout the year than you did with your own family members. When things are uncomfortable at work, it begins to spill over into your family and work life. Let's look at how this can happen in these reconstructed examples:

- You start mentioning the person's name and the problem they have created in your work space as soon as you get home

- Daily phone conversations to family and friends begin with, "Guess what *she* did today?"

- Nightly dinner conversations at home begin with, "I hate going to work….or she is making me miserable"

- Every day you dread going into the same shared office space and seeing the person; you make every effort to go in the opposite direction

- When the person asks you a question at work, you pretend that you don't know the answer and direct them to others who really don't know the answer either

- When the person asks you about things they should already know at work, you tell them you haven't heard anything so that you can avoid having further conversations with them altogether

- You begin to eat your lunch at work in isolation near the utility closets

- You begin to talk to other people at work you really don't like to ensure that you will be engaged in conversation should the person happen to show up

- You go to your boss about the issue after realizing that you should have worked this one out yourself; now it looks like you can't work with others and problem solve on your own

Alexa, Hold Up On My New iPhone

Employers shouldn't hear or see you hovered over your cell phone all day at work or walking around with the latest buds stuffed in your ears. You should be actively engaged at work and productive at all times. So what do we do with the smokers and vapers who take 15 breaks a day to feed their nicotine habits? In some work places, employers have decided not to hire smokers because long breaks often lead to poor job performance and low productivity.

To monitor staff, many employers are installing cameras in the staff lounge, conference rooms, offices, hall ways, parking lots, main entrances, lobbies, cafeterias and back door entrances to see what employees are really doing during work hours. Pending on the work load, some companies prefer limited conversations with other employees to ensure mass production to meet customer satisfaction, especially if the job is physical labor around the clock. If caught on too many breaks, a verbal warning could be issued followed by a write up and supervisor meeting. Check on the company's cell phone policy to find out expectations for productivity while at work and during scheduled lunch times. The next time you are at work, take a look around the workplace. You might be surprised at how many people are on their cell phones during the course of an 8-hour work day.

Technology All Around Us

We all know that you cannot look at inappropriate websites on the computer at work, yet we sign this company waiver understanding the ramifications of violating this important policy. So why do so many people still cross the line at the work place? Technology can be a curse or a blessing, depending on how it is used. Today's society relies on their cell phone, iPad, laptop, drone, webcam, Smartwatch, and Apple computer so heavily that if they leave it home or forget it some place, they would never survive the day. If you look around, everyone's head is in the "down" position reading an electronic device. *They never look up.*

I was on the train the other day, and the door didn't self-close when it began to move. I sat in the middle and counted how many minutes it would take for someone to notice the loud noise and 35 degree wind that blew in on our faces. The woman who was in the front seat kept looking up to see the opened door but would not shut it. Another man glanced up to see the open door, but would not get up to close it. The other passenger who was directly in front of the door, simply contained her annoyed face regarding the situation but did not move. Finally, an elderly gentleman and myself got up at the same time and asked everyone in unison, "How long was every one going to sit and not shut the door?" He beat me to the punch and our puzzled faces simply could not comprehend what just happened. The cold gusts of wind and the noise was unbearable. Even after the door was finally closed, no one even cared enough to notice our frustrated plight.

At the next stop, the door did not self-close again and we waited to see who would be the hero or heroine in this next play scene. Again, no one got up to close the door after five minutes so a young woman angrily got up to close the door. Technology had everyone engulfed in their morning routine and the wintry air had gone unnoticed…just a simple tightening of a scarf or pulling up a hood to stay warm seemed to be the only recourse for the change in temperature. It dawned on me that technology was more important than being observant to solve the easiest problem of all: simply closing a train door to protect us all from the blustery cold winds.

Although today's technology is very advanced, it simply cannot perform this one task: *teach us plain old common sense, sensitivity and genuine compassion for others.* For example, on the train a huge reconstructed sign reads:

PLEASE SAVE THESE SEATS FOR <u>SENIORS</u> AND <u>PHYSICALLY CHALLENGED</u> PASSENGERS

You can't be more specific than this. Seats are saved specifically for the visually impaired, physically disabled, challenged or blind. Yet, when these passengers come aboard, "regular able bodied people" are camped out in these reserved seats tied down to electronic devices oblivious to the passenger who is out of breath helplessly holding on to their cane for balance and desperately searching for a seat nearby. As the train sways back and forth, these passengers just want to rest after such a concerted effort boarding those steep steps. **DID ANY ONE READ THE SIGN?** Sadly, very few offer the seat that's supposed to be reserved for them in the first place. I'm glad that the conductors monitor this situation at every stop.

I guess I miss good old-fashioned kindness and chivalry for our human race. Young mothers with children and strollers have the same issue and it's disheartening to see it play out. The blind and the deaf experience the same, especially those passengers who require a guide dog or walking stick to help them along to their destinations. The train door is very heavy and even I struggle to open it myself. My eyes darted for a gentleman to help me, but I couldn't make eye contact or get his attention because his head was down mesmerized in the cell phone glow. When I raised my voice to get help, still no one budged until I tapped on a broad shoulder. I finally got the man's attention to look up and see what was going on. That simple tap scared the man half out of his wits because he did not notice that I was in such close proximity.

Most of us will attempt to advocate for people in wheelchairs waiting to enter the elevator but sadly no one moves to help them inside or gets out of the way when they try to exit. Again, there's the posted reconstructed big red sign:

ATTENTION:
Wheelchairs Must Enter
and Exit Elevator First

To learn more about the U.S. Supreme Court's decision on self-advocacy and disability rights in your state, please visit www.olmsteadrights.org.

Did you Know that.....

...most people look at their cell phones at least 125 times a day?

...40 million Americans have a disability and need assistance walking, seeing or living independently?

...Americans with disabilities are less likely to use technology?

...10,000 people turn 65 ever day in the United States?

...more and more workplaces are requiring employees to take mandatory disability and discriminatory professional development workshops to maintain employment?

...since so many employees are on their cell phones, work productivity has decreased over the last decade?

...basic social skills are worsening since more people are becoming isolated in their homes as a result of playing video games, streaming movies/free television, online ordering and express meal delivery?

WORD of the Day: PRAXEOLOGY—the study of human conduct

Your Turn Activity:

1. Today's world is sometimes unkind. **Write down 5 things you could do to make it a better place for someone who is a senior or physically challenged.**

   a. ____

   b. ____

   c. ____

   d. ____

   e. ____

2. Have someone tie a scarf or long sock to cover your eyes. **For 30 minutes, try to do 3 things you normally would do if you could see.** Try to do these 3 activities around the house. In the spaces below, write down how many minutes it took to complete the task:

   __________ Pick out an outfit to wear for an interview

   __________ Make a peanut butter and jelly sandwich

   __________ Walk to the mailbox and pick up the mail

3. **Invite 5 people over for an informal backyard barbecue.** Mix up the crowd a little but also invite the following:

   +   Someone everyone likes and is humorous

   +   Someone who likes to help and serve others

   -     Someone who is always late and complains

   -     Someone who talks a lot and offers advice

   ++   Someone who just eats and doesn't mingle

After the party, talk with your best friend about how the event went over all and what you learned about the different personalities. Would you invite the same people again? Why or why not?

____

____

____

Chapter 9 Notes

Chapter 9 Notes

Step 10: Learn to write with self-confidence to communicate effectively with professionals in your chosen career to compete in the global workforce.

Chapter 10

First-Year College: Can "One Size fit All?"

Yo, What's Up Teach?

High School mentality vs. College reality now comes down to maturity and communication to professionals such as advisors, professors and financial conversations that can determine if higher learning is the best academic route for students who test below college level courses.

Today's College Student Prototype

I've taught kindergarten to college over the last 20 years. As an adjunct instructor teaching on the college and university levels, I've witnessed student behavior that still leaves me aghast this very day. High school starts the development of maturity, self-confidence, time management, work ethics and most of all respect for authority especially those who have the passion and stamina to teach others. College culminates learning concepts learned in high school which completes the entire K-12 academic process. However, along the way fuzzy educational vertical lines appear on the television interrupted by a national service announcement to stay tuned for academic emergency instructions.

Here are some reconstructed commercial breaks that have disrupted my classroom performed by students who just graduated high school entering college for the first time or returned after several years with little or no college experience:

Prototype #1: The Sports Athlete

No student schedule. Just ear buds blasting loud music as they pass by other students and settle down in a seat far, far in the back of the classroom. When the door closes and class begins, they continue to concentrate on dreaming of the day to sign a professional sports contract with championship bonuses attached. When the music finally stops, sporty unrealistic expectations turn around and walk out the door.

Prototype #2: Friday Night Special

It was a long night. The college parking lot sports rented luxury cars, coupes and stretch limo Jeeps with burnt orange leather seats in black trim. As class starts and grand late entrances are made, verbal frenzy happens in the center aisle. Shouldn't everyone be given an A as soon as possible since it's so early? How annoying to expect hard work and class participation on a Saturday morning.

Prototype #3: The Leather Jacket

Only cool dudes can wear black leather jackets in the summer time with the sleeves pushed up. It never comes off no matter how hot or cold the room temperature. It is a signature jacket that no one else can have while in the same classroom. Since it was summer, the heat began to rise in the classroom and the signature jacket finally came off and settled in on the back of the Instructor's chair. It was marveled by everyone in the course.

Prototype # 4: The Body Builder

Instructors always know when there will be trouble. When the roster fell short of celebrity names, an up and coming body builder stood in the doorway. A five o'clock shadow and wavy blonde hair sent the young ladies in an uproar! Somehow without the Instructor's permission, the classroom turned into a local bar and serious competition for a certain phone number after class. It was the first time so many eager female students took an educational interest in "community-based learning" in a course.

Prototype #5: The Genius

Every topic has a slant that can only be explained from this acquired intellect and point of view. An IQ of 140 is excellent, but a 160 is among the cosmic stars. Who could compete with a genius? Just a dandy college policy manual highlighting student codes of conduct for their reading enjoyment. Genius.

Prototype #6: The Bionic Cell Phone

The cell phone policy is always introduced on the first day of class. The "No Cell Phone" sign was posted in three places in the classroom and introduced during the college policy discussion. Then, it rang during the video presentation. It rang during the mini-lecture. The phone was answered each time and a sunny conversation started shortly after. At last it was finally put away, but only to pulsate on vibrate. It caused so much disruption that it needed back up intervention. It was finally confiscated since it could not be put away and would not give up ringing. The phone was i-Bionic with special powers.

Prototype #7: The Recluse

Seated in the last row of the class sat someone who would not raise a hand when called during attendance. No sudden moves to participate in the group discussion. Complete refusal to pair with a partner. The hoodie would not come off and requests to sign-in were ignored. There's just something about a corner wall that's warm and inviting.

Prototype #8: The Caveman

That's the way we did it 20 years ago. Now they invent a hybrid course (part online/part face-to-face instruction) and must meet the required course prerequisites. How do you turn on the computer? How do you log-on or log-off? It was nearly impossible to navigate any computer learning program without getting completely lost.

Prototype #9: The Soap Nurse

Profanity could actually have its own dialect. Every sentence had a bad word that needed bleeping out for the sake of the course syllabus and ministers registered for class. If there was a bar of soap nearby, that mouth could be washed out squeaky clean. Can you imagine what bleeps at work to patients who accidently soil their hospital gowns?

Prototype #10: Let's Make a Deal

We know when a deal maker enters a classroom. Chipper, smiling and shaking everyone's hand way too hard. Holds the most trophies for debate teams and is way ahead of the Instructor's introduction. There's a debate on every assignment, every grade earned and any movie about a debate. All class assignments must be completed. This is a very big deal.

Prototype #11: More English, Por Favor

Some students can speak up to four languages though it may be hard to interpret or understand the entire conversation. Since practice makes perfect in any language, most groups are paired together in courses to orally present a final project in English. With daily practice, English also becomes easier to communicate to others although it may be their second language.

Prototype #12: The 80 year-old Freshman

At some colleges and universities, tuition is free when you are over the age of 65. And they are good scholars, too. They work hard to turn in fabulous papers, go above and beyond in assignments and can rattle on for 45 minutes on a 10-minute presentation. They arrive 30 minutes early for class and hang around after class, too. No one's in a big hurry. After all, they are retired and have all the time in the world.

Prototype #13: Extra Credit Mantras

In high school, extra credit is issued to prevent completely flunking a class. In college, you simply have to do the work, come to class and pass your exams. You can only earn an A, B, C or F; the letter "D" doesn't exist on an interim report card at the college level. It's the law of college nature. It is also not fair to students who have consistently been in class, submitted work on time and participated to earn a passing grade.

Prototype #14: The Borrower

There's no paper, pen, pencil, notebook or book bag. They just don't have any supplies of their own. Yours look so much better. Your paper is of good quality and your pens are the best on the market. And by the end of the class, your brand new supplies are mysteriously gone. Every week they like to "borrow" what they need and for some odd reason, they also forget to give "your" own supplies back.

On the Road to College Success: Oral Presentation Shakes at Stake

At some point in your college career, an oral presentation will be required as part of your grade. In some instances, this can weight up to 40% of the overall grade. Procrastination is for "pros" who earn their living procrastinating. It's what they do and can do it on a professional level. So when the Instructor says to practice in the mirror for an amount of time given, you can bet that this time will not change on the presentation day. Some people just have a fear of speaking in front of others since it may cause anxiety and stress that raises blood pressure in a matter of minutes.

Ollie was next in line to present. It was so overwhelming that when his name was called, he dramatically ran out. Another student covered her face and burst into tears while still in her seat. Another young man's chin was quivering and looked at me like a scared puppy. I've never seen this much anxiety and disruption in the years that I've been teaching. I discovered that they did not have oral presentations in any of their high school courses. As a result, two students failed the class because they were too scared to present in front of their peers that day. It was only a **5** minute presentation!

Earning College Credits

College grading is a little different from high school. First of all, the letter "D" does not hang out in a college classroom and will not appear on an interim report card. In high school, the letter "D" lives everywhere in the school hallways and signifies a passing grade in a core subject. In college, it represents just the opposite: if you have earned a "C" in the course, it may mean that you need extra academic support to retain the course material. Anything lower than a "C" becomes a failing grade since the "D" does not exist at this level. It may also be difficult to pass the final exam pending on how it's weighted. Here are a few tips to pass a college course on your own:

- *Arrive on time and sit in the front*—hiding in the back row just increases your risk for miscommunication for important assignment instructions. Sitting in the front decreases phone distractions, side bar conversations and student disruptions. Instructors don't like to keep repeating things when you are not paying attention. This is particularly important when assignments are given and you have missed important steps on how to respond in Discussion Board.

- *Get your textbook early*—don't wait until the last minute when the line is wrapped around the corner! Professors want the required book in class and on time. Be smart and don't tear off the plastic shrink wrap just yet. If the textbook will not be used, then you can return it to the bookstore and get a full refund. If the original wrap is torn or missing, it will considered a "used" textbook and maybe 50% will be refunded, but not guaranteed. Plan ahead and get the textbook in case it is out of stock. You just might get an assignment that requires reading a chapter before the first class and counts as your first graded assignment.

- *Introduce yourself to classmates*—this is a great way to exchange information in case one of you misses class and can later share notes to catch up. When you get to know your classmates, you'll be surprised at the plethora of resources pooled together to benefit one another. This is how study groups are formed, lasting friendships begin and networking can lead to that dream job by simply meeting the right people.

- *Turn in assignments before the due date*—don't wait until the last minute because things can happen beyond your control to prevent getting the assignment completed. Start right after class when it's still fresh in your memory. This way if you still have questions, you can find out the Instructor's office hours for clarification. Trying to send e-mails asking for clarification the day before an assignment is due runs a risk of getting a late response 24 hours later.

- *Ask for academic support when you earn "C's" on quizzes and exams*—if you are studying and this is your best grade, it's time to reach out for help in understanding material that might be more difficult than you expected

- *Know the Instructor's office hours*—this is a great time to get to know your professor and build an educational relationship. If you are struggling in the class, now's the time to schedule an appointment and talk about strategies to help you pass the course. Since Instructors have many courses and students, it's easier for them to remember you when you come to them in person.

- *Don't skip class*—when you are not there, all work turns into a "0" with limited time to make it up. You really can't get a grade for something if you are not physically there in attendance. Also, tests are crucial and need to be worked out with the Test Center and your Instructor.

- *Send an e-mail when you are absent*—this shows the Instructor that not only do you care, but you have a logical reason which prevented you from attending. Absences require proof such as a doctor's note (urgent care center, hospital, etc.) which confirms your return back to school. If you had a flat tire, bring the receipt from the repair. If you were in an accident, bring a copy of the police report. If you attended a funeral, bring a copy of the program. Documentation to the Instructor shows that you are sincere and the situation really did happen.

Getting on the Road to College Success: Writing Right

One of the requirements in college is *writing*. It doesn't go away. Writing is required in every single course subject—even math! If writing is not your absolute favorite, then DO NOT PASS GO and forfeit your $200. Instead, visit the college's Writing Center for assistance and brush up on rusty areas that may include:

- Grammar

- Punctuation

- Confusing words

- Run-Ons

- Fragments

- Comma Splices

- Adjectives

- Adverbs

- Sentences (simple, compound and complex)

- Sentence Types (declarative, imperative, exclamatory and interrogative)

- Thesis (in beginning of first paragraph)

- Re-stated Thesis (found in conclusion)

- Abstracts

- Summaries

- MLA and APA formats

- Research Paper references

- Arguments

- Poor Writing in America (See Chapter 1)

- Oral presentations (see page 97 for sample rubric)

Study Strategies & Notetaking

It's so hard to read 40 pages of a college textbook let alone take notes on what you've just read! Most study strategies involve studying the night before in the wee hours of 3 a.m. with power drinks and tons of coffee and Mountain Dew to stay awake. Instead of planning ahead and working backwards to the test date, some students end up failing the test.

First, let's look at how you might take notes. During class, the Instructor will emphasize main ideas, important concepts, new terms, and cover all course material you should know. Here is a reconstructed example of an English class notes written on loose leaf paper using the red lined margin and ==highlighted== to show main ideas set up in the Cornell Notes format:

John Salami, Jr. 4/12/17	English 402	Instructor: Mr. Bologna N. Cheeze
Researching Topics on Meats	==Use reliable sources== such as library journals & magazines, interviews, university studies, and experts—stay away from internet and Google searches	
Writing a Thesis on processed meat	Use 5 W's to create a good sentence (who, what, where, when, why) This should be the overall summary; should ==hook the reader== and appear in the last sentence of the introductory paragraph	
Vocabulary Sandwich Test	Coming up on 4/20; ==Review and study pages 23-47== in textbook. Complete all unit tests. Type up text responses and e-mail to Instructor by 4/17	
Begin Research Topic:	Why Americans love hotdogs, scrapple and Spam. Use information discussing ==modern day== factories and production, ingredients that cause cancer and why we should read product labels	
Next class: oral presentation on topic selected and	Give 3 reasons for choice and share research you've found so far ==Rubric 10+ minutes=A==; 8 minutes= B; 6 minutes= C; 5 minutes= D; 4 minutes=F ==(this will be counted as a quiz grade)==	
its importance (10 minute time limit)	must include introduction and conclusion with Q & A at end NOTE: *Remember not to fidget during my presentation!*	

For test-taking strategies, follow these 10 rules for a better academic outcome:

1. **Find out the test date early and plan backwards**—if the test is on the 15th, start studying on the first to begin retaining and memorizing the information

2. **Review quizzes and classwork**—look at instructor comments and feedback; find out timeframe given for test (whole class period, 1 hour, 15 minutes, etc.)

3. **Review the study guide**—break it down in sections: vocabulary, concepts, and formulas; select a section to study every morning which is the best time to retain information

4. **Make up your own test or quiz**—put all information in multiple choice, written response and fill in the blank; use flash cards terminology and important dates

5. **Find a study group**—it's better with two or more people for valued input, information you may have missed and overall support to make test less overwhelming and stressful

6. **Get a good night's rest the night before**—don't try to cram because your body will be tired and your brain will be working overtime to recall the jumbled information

7. **Spend the night** <u>reviewing</u> **not studying**—the hard work has already been done over the last two weeks; concentrate on skimming/scanning and reviewing vocabulary

8. **On day of the test, eat a good breakfast**—protein foods (egg whites, peanut butter, oatmeal) and fresh fruit (bananas, apples) get the brain ready for recalling information

9. **Arrive early**—don't arrive stressed because you overslept or got caught in traffic. Get a seat in the front so you don't miss any important test instructions

10. **Pace yourself**—don't rush! Skim over the test first and answer the easy parts. If you have to respond, remember to write legible and elaborate to earn more points

In the Nick of Time

So, what do you do in 24 hours? We all get the same amount of time, but what matters is *how we spend it.* For example, if you only get four hours of sleep per night what are you doing for the rest of the day? My guess is that you are exhausted, irritable and sometimes forgetful of basic things you know as a routine. Everything becomes a chore: driving, sitting in traffic, waiting in line, running errands, getting dressed, preparing for work or anything that requires some sort of *physical* effort on your behalf. On the other hand, if you are constantly making decisions, reviewing paperwork, booking your calendar or planning activities then this takes on a *mental* strain on your brain and even it must take a rest.

For some, *emotional* stress can be detrimental, too when you constantly worry, overthink situations or take on other people's problems.

Today's world carries an electronic device in their hand or snapped on a wrist and requires a different kind of effort: *constantly looking down 90% of the day causing harmful eye and neck strain.* Our bodies call for rest, especially if you continue on 12-15 hour days. Most people sleep with their phones by the night stand "just in case" someone sends an important message by way of text, e-mail, screenshot, video, download, picture, or voicemail that can't be missed.

You've probably haven't given much thought to what you really do within a 24-hour day until now. Let's look at the ***Time Management Worksheet Chart* on the next page.** It's divided into 24 squares so that you can put your daily activities from the time you wake up until the time you go to bed. Next, **complete the Quiz** that follows. You are going to be surprised at the number of points you earn and how you manage your time.

You've Got 24 Hours!

<table>
<tr><td></td><td></td><td></td><td></td></tr>
<tr><td></td><td></td><td></td><td></td></tr>
<tr><td></td><td></td><td></td><td></td></tr>
<tr><td></td><td></td><td></td><td></td></tr>
<tr><td></td><td></td><td></td><td></td></tr>
<tr><td></td><td></td><td></td><td></td></tr>
</table>

Each box represents 1 hour. Write how you spend **24 hours.** (Ex: Sleeping 8 hours fills 8 boxes) Other activities may include interacting on social media, driving, eating out, working, exercising, taking care of others, studying, playing sports, time on computer, etc.

How do I manage my time?
Take the Quiz below to find out!

1 Not at all   2 Not really   3 Sometimes   4 Often   5 Very Often

1. Is your office or work space organized at home?   1 2 3 4 5
2. Is your office or department organized at your place of work?   1 2 3 4 5
3. Do you complete tasks at the last minute?   1 2 3 4 5
4. Do you set aside time for weekly planning and scheduling?   1 2 3 4 5
5. Do you pack lunch, lay out clothes & find keys to ready for next day?   1 2 3 4 5
6. How much time is spent on dealing with interruptions?   1 2 3 4 5
7. Do you use goal setting strategies to decide which task to work on?   1 2 3 4 5
8. Do you leave extra time for unexpected situations and traffic?   1 2 3 4 5
9. Do you begin your tasks with high, medium or low priority?   1 2 3 4 5
10. When given a new assignment, do you start right away?   1 2 3 4 5
11. When deadlines and commitments are mentioned, do you stress out?   1 2 3 4 5
12. Do you take work home to get it done in time for the next day?   1 2 3 4 5
13. Do you write down a daily "to-do" list?   1 2 3 4 5
14. Do you confirm priorities with your boss or teacher?   1 2 3 4 5
15. Do you over commit to tasks without checking your availability?   1 2 3 4 5
16. Do you find financial deadlines or due dates stressful?   1 2 3 4 5
17. Do you ask for help or support when you feel overwhelmed?   1 2 3 4 5
18. Do you like to manage multiple tasks at a time?   1 2 3 4 5
19. Do you keep a daily planner or agenda book?   1 2 3 4 5
20. How much time do you spend watching t.v. and on social media?   1 2 3 4 5

69-100 Points = You are a great time manager and can help others!

35-68 Points = You are good, but there's still some wiggle room for improvement

0-34 Points = Time to start serious time management strategies at work & school

So what did you spend your time doing? Circle any of the activities below:

- Preparing for work in the morning
- Commuting to work or taking the bus
- Watching television
- Preparing breakfast, lunch and dinner
- Playing video games
- Watching movies
- Running errands
- Sleeping
- Exercising
- Playing sports
- Pampering yourself (massage, haircut, salon, etc.)
- Working overtime
- Social activities (movies, time with friends, going out, etc.)
- Eating out
- Community Work
- Caregiver for small children or elderly
- Laundry
- Bathing and hygiene
- Cleaning the house
- Yardwork
- Washing/cleaning the car
- Washing dishes
- Grocery shopping
- Picking up prescriptions/health and wellness products
- Attending sporting events
- Talking on the phone or texting
- Writing, drawing or taking pictures
- Studying

- Reading
- Favorite hobby

This is probably just scratching the surface, but how often do you set time aside for lunch while at work? For dinner, do you cook and enjoy your meal or do you eat fast food while driving? You will be surprised to learn how quickly 24 hours goes by: the week seems like a blur until Friday and then the weekend somehow speeds up skidding right into Sunday night.

Why does everyone dread early Monday morning blues? Talk about how time flies!

The hardest part about time management for most students is *daily interruptions*. There are phone messages, text messages, e-mail messages, and hours spent on social media. If you work at an office, some disruptions need immediate attention such copy machine toner or paper refills and the classic: someone left it jammed and now its blinking like a Christmas tree for you to fix it. If you don't, it leaves your own copy job on hold which turns into *one more* interruption during your work day.

Time management can easily and quickly slip away from us each day. The way we handle time is what determines what gets done in 24 hours and how we can schedule our week. Most of us get caught up with putting too much on our plate and spreading ourselves too thin. Even though students dislike agenda books, day timers and planners, they can help combat time obstacles and prevent over commitment to other events or activities that simply cannot fit into the weekly schedule—no matter how badly we want it on the calendar! Here are some gentle "NO" phrases that can help put some of that time back into your week:

- *"I'd love to but I really can't right now"*

- *"Thank you for including me but I'm going to decline this time"*

- *"I'd like to but I am already working on A, B & C right now"*

- *"Follow up with me again in a few weeks when things slow down"*

- *"Before I commit to this, let me check my calendar first"*

If you stick to it, people will understand and respect you for being honest and not over committing yourself to only let them down later when they really need you the most.

After completing the *Time Management Worksheet*, were you surprised by what it revealed on paper? How did you really spend time and with whom? If it's valuable time wasted, it should help you make critical changes especially if you are not taking care of yourself or spending too much time on things that aren't helping you reach or set realistic career, family or personal goals. You'll also find that **if you don't take the time to start planning for the future, it will pass you by just as quickly as yesterday**, last week, last month and last year. Time flies even faster when you are having the time of your life and yet when we think of tough, sad or transitional situations that caused us hardships, time just seemed to creep on by.

Think about when you were in kindergarten to where you are now. It goes even faster when you have children. That saying, "*Time waits for no man*" really is true. Look at where you want to be and what you want to accomplish in your lifetime. It all starts with how you manage your time. "*Don't put off tomorrow what you can do today.*" Everyone gets the same 24 hours every day. Have you thought about what you will do with yours? Let's look at how time effects the educational process. Every student starts out with an "A," but the key is how many will keep it or end up failing based on time management choices.

Strategies for Passing Classes

There are 4 P's in Passing college courses:

1. **Participation**—come to class and arrive on time; chime in for class discussions

2. **Pen Pals**—get to know the person sitting beside you, in front of you and in back of you

3. **Projects**—start them early when assigned on first day and understand the rubrics and requirements

4. **Presentations**—practice public speaking in front of an audience of your peers and co-workers for at least 15 minutes

Failing Classes: No Strategy Required

The Biggest P of them all: PROCRASTINATION! When we talk about famous celebrity athletes, who comes to mind when these sports icons are mentioned? Fill in the blanks below with your favorite picks:

Basketball   _______________________________

Baseball   _______________________________

Bowling   _______________________________

Cycling   _______________________________

Football   _______________________________

Golf   _______________________________

Gymnastics   _______________________________

Ice Hockey   _______________________________

NASCAR   _______________________________

Soccer   _______________________________

Swimming   _______________________________

Tennis   _______________________________

Track & Field   _______________________________

UFC   _______________________________

Volleyball   _______________________________

Wrestling   _______________________________

Some athletes became famous because of their will and drive to be the best in the world and daily practice. But students have created a new kind of PRO starting in middle school infiltrating through high school with putting important things off (**procrastinating**) until the last minute. The easiest way to fail in college is to keep putting off the assignment or exam and *hoping* for the best outcome. Professors <u>know the difference between real time and effort</u> vs. <u>just finished it this morning</u>. Especially if your project looks like it had a fight in the car and your wrinkled outfit did not recover from the commotion.

Course Requirements: Rubric and Syllabus Go Together

In today's college expectations for success, it is important to understand what you signed up for. Whether you take the course online, hybrid (face-to-face and online), or face-to-face with an Instructor, the first thing that will be covered is the syllabus. It has the college logo on it, the Instructor's name, course number and days/time it plans to meet. Further down it lists the "do's and don'ts" of the class such as lateness, absences, misconduct, college policies, course expectations and what you will learn (objectives). Most importantly, it tells you what is required to pass the course along with a suggested grading or point system.

Now the **rubric** is equally important because it gives the road map to the grade you are trying to achieve in the class. For example, if you have to write an English paper, the requirement might be 5 pages. The rubric will break down in a category point system in which the paper is scored to give you an idea of how the Instructor will use the rubric to come up with your projected grade. Here's a reconstructed rubric example:

Grade A	Grade B	Grade C	Grade F
Excellent written paper; completed 5 pages, stayed on topic	**Very good** written paper; completed 5 pages, stayed on topic	**Developing** written paper; completed 3-4 pages, topic unclear	**Poorly written** paper; completed 1-2 pages, roamed off topic

Included well-developed outline; well written introduction and thesis	Included developed outline; good introduction and thesis	Included under developed outline; introduction and thesis is developing	Included a portion of the outline; hard to follow introduction and/or thesis
No grammatical errors	1-2 grammatical errors	3-4 grammatical errors	5 or more grammatical errors

Meeting Department Advisors

In college degree programs, things change all the time: the department chair, the adjunct professors, the text book editions, and of course the advisors. Sometimes there are two or three advisors in the same department. To keep on top of course requirements and ensure that you graduate on time, follow these simple steps:

- Print a copy of your course schedule

- Send an e-mail to introduce yourself (include your Student ID# and use the name printed on your course schedule)

- Set up a time to meet (check Instructor posted office hours)

- Locate your program department and advisor

- Gather any questions about your program that might need clarification

If you don't get a response within the week, take a walk over to the department. This is very important in the beginning of your program. Since changes happen often and quickly, it helps to know who to talk to and what courses may be needed or have been deleted from the program degree.

Professor Communication: Improves Your Academic Relation

It's tough when your parents come with you to college for the first time. First stop is where to park the car without getting a campus ticket. Next, finding the main lobby entrance and pretending to understand complicated directions to the Admissions Office from the front desk. When the student is asked a question, both parents answer simultaneously with folded arms anticipating the next question with raised eyebrows of apprehension. Some students listen, dart wide-eyes to and from strangers who pass by, and are just thankful that someone knows how to speak College Jargon 101.

But what happens when parents are not there to guide and answer questions about financial aid, campus resources and the course syllabus? The college professor is also a wealth of information and communication is the major key to understanding and passing college courses. Students learn to advocate for themselves and develop communication through the professor. For example, if the student arrives late and the course syllabus does not allow late entries into the class after the door is shut, this needs to be addressed during the Professor's office hours. Banging on the door or jumping up and down to see through the narrow door window during class will only aggravate the situation even more. Another example could be texting on your cell phone when signs have been posted in the classroom followed by defined college policies that do not allow constant talking and disruptions during class lecture.

Students quickly learn that all Professors are different: some friendly, some aloof, some just await for retirement while others do not wish to be bothered except during posted office hours only. Word quickly gets around which Professor to take and which courses to drop or add. At the larger universities, professors are rated by the students which determines why some courses fill up more quickly than others.

For newcomers to the college world, it's important to learn some basic rules of when and how to eloquently communicate to your Professor and other professionals on campus. This also gives parents who might not realize the class rules of etiquette a better appreciation of what many Professors experience in both community college and university levels. These golden rules are great analogies of a Professors' prenuptial agreement before officially getting married to your college degree:

- You must attend and pass all of your courses

- You must stay informed of program changes in your major

- You must meet with your advisor regularly

- You must read ALL of the fine print on admissions forms as well as other documents you sign with your program Advisor

And just like a real marriage, academic success can determine if your two or four year tenure will last. In any degree, getting along with Professors and following the college policies will get you the 411 on how to keep the honeymoon going until you walk down the aisle with a college diploma in hand. Most importantly, you'll be ahead of your peers and have no regrets for what others did inappropriately in and out of class before you came along.

Did you know that.......

…most new students in their first year of college do not read the college policies handbook?

…many college freshmen do not pass the Reading, Writing and Math assessment and start on the remedial level in college?

…taking a career assessment in high school and college helps to determine the type of occupation that matches up skill sets, knowledge and technology?

……most millennials carry or own at least 3 electronic devices and purchase the latest and often the most expensive cell phones, ear buds or ear phones?

…many teen students seldom patronize the library, do not know the library's range of services and do not participate in the library's summer reading programs that offer major prizes?

…..most high schools give mandatory summer reading assignments (often classic novels) that are due the first day of school and count as a grade?

…..summer reading promotes literacy, develops vocabulary and helps retain skills during the summer break?

……many scholarships are not awarded because students simply do not apply?

WORD of the Day: CHRONOLOGY—a report, description or account of an event or situation

Your Turn Activity:

1. **Put together a report about your week.** Note the most important points for each day. (For example: attended awards banquet for son, family ate dinner together, new college course started, etc.)

Sunday	
Monday	
Tuesday	
Wednesday	
Thursday	
Friday	
Saturday	

2. **Think of a class or course that you failed (D or F) in high school or college (F).** What could you have done better? How did you feel seeing it on your transcript? What do you know **now** that you wish you could have done then? Respond to what applies to your situation below:

I really should have spent more time:

Studying	Because
Managing my time	Because
Communicating with Instructor	Because
Other reasons	As a result,

3. **What do you want to be when you grow up?** Think about what you said when you were in elementary school and where you are now. Is it still the same? If not, where do you see yourself in the next 5-10 years?

When I was little I wanted to be:	(Occupation/Job)
Now, I see myself as a:	(Occupation/Career)

Chapter 10 Notes

Chapter 10 Notes

Epilogue

This book was solely created to help parents, students, coaches, athletes, ESL learners, professionals and especially **college freshmen** to navigate through today's complex education system. Over the past 20 years, I've watched the educational process crumble into a myriad of complexities which have resulted in more and more students wanting out of the system after high school. When I learned of the dropout rate for Delaware students in 2018, 699 was far too many who gave up on the education system for whatever reason or situation. I can only imagine how many dropped out in the other 49 United States. For those who wanted to attend college, starting at the remedial course level is a clear indication of the educational system failing them. As a result, so many students are getting left behind.....

Since being in the Education arena, I've learned a monumental lesson: ***most students do not like to read and write***. Technology is taking over more than we realize—students struggle with being creative in the classroom and rely on Google and hover over their cell phone during class time. When I provide *Sign-In Sheets* at my workshops and classes, I am not surprised anymore that cell phones have become the student's identity and legible handwriting a lost art. I simply can't decipher anyone's written name—it's part cursive, part print or part scratched in. If this is the new "normal" then legibility has to be retaught. After all, you simply must sign your John Hancock in this day and age.

From Kindergarten to Kollege in 10 Steps offers parents and students a true resource to navigate through our complex education system with humor and light heartedness to make education terminology easier to understand. Since education is such a serious topic, this book becomes a necessary tool and resource for **any** household that needs **support in the school or college classroom**. Many parents have come to me with their hands thrown up and worn out from academic misfires trying to help with homework, understanding report cards and getting the help they need in Special Education. Hopefully as you've read through each chapter, there was an area of interest that helped with understanding specific areas of our educational system: pre-school, elementary, middle, high school and college. Not only is education a major concern for a child's future, but other aspects include understanding the dynamics of diversity and inclusion, workplace preparation, utilizing the Common Core State Standards, interpreting report cards, and gaining a crystal clear overview of grades K-12 expectations through graduation. If a child is falling behind, <u>teachers who really care about your child will offer resources for academic support.</u> You might not want to hear it, but the decision you make after that can make or break that child's love for learning. *Academic support starts out like a retirement plan*: it only gets expensive as you get older and inflation makes it nearly impossible to compound your 2% rate in two years instead of starting 10 years ago when it could have grown over time.

Everyone has their own views on the perils of our education system, but I wanted parents and students to see it through my eyes since trends continue to change throughout the United States. I still believe that **some basic aspects of *Old Skool* teaching can still work** and be utilized in our classrooms today. Many of my students who had IEP's, learning disabilities, behavioral problems or speech impediments related to my unique methods of teaching. The secret? Good old-fashioned tender loving care (TLC)! It sounds so basic but it is really true! Behaviors improve, learning disabilities reach higher levels and speech impediments are a matter of language practice, repeat of sounds and sight words. When students see that you really care about them and are true to your word, their world of trust opens up. We could only guess what goes on at home after school is out so when they are with us, it becomes important to get to know them, teach them and provide them with needed resources when they reach out for our assistance.

This book is meant to help **college freshmen students and athletes** navigate through academics and expected athletic performances every season. Freshmen orientation is the first major step from graduating high school while college schedules and accountability marks yet another milestone to the finish line of completing a degree and competing globally into the real world. College freshmen need guidance and academic resources to continue learning in this new environment which requires time management skills, academic support and social media accountabilities. This is why the **activities were put at the end of each chapter:** to practice critical thinking skills. Seems basic, but learning took place while reading the chapter and quizzes (recalling of information and understanding) were given to measure the outcome. Instructors can also modify lessons according to student grade levels.

For athletic coaches, this book can serve as a resource to navigate athletes into a new dimension of balancing academics with athletics. College evolves around eligibility in the NCAA and other Division II and Division III schools. Just as they practice to be the best on the basketball court or football field, academics must be practiced as well. Continuous motivation and monitoring is the key to a holistic athlete. I know. I played and it is hard work earning award recognition and division conference titles while keeping up grades to stay on the team when the coach needs you the most. Great athletes are expected to maintain that high level of athleticism in sports competition while balancing textbooks in the other hand. That's why fans like buzzer beaters—it showcases true athletic talent throughout the country and coaches must maintain team eligibility year after year.

For adult learners and professionals, <u>vocabulary</u> plays a huge role in the way we work together, prepare students for college and thrive in the global workforce. It was taught and learned in my favorite *Dick and Jane* first leveled reader book and continues throughout the college process. For **ESL learners**, it becomes very important to quickly learn our language to hold jobs and navigate through our complex educational system. This book can also serve as a s guide to anyone who did not receive academic support in their early years of learning. Whether you dropped out of high school, experienced college but didn't graduate, or worked your way up through the ranks as a professional, some students have come face-to-face with the following educational barriers:

- Gave up on the school system
- Could not find the right fit in resources available
- Felt too prideful or embarrassed to accept academic support
- Could not afford academic tutoring
- Was afraid or embarrassed to ask questions or get clarifications
- Felt unworthy of receiving academic support
- A teacher or educator was uncaring or discouraging
- Did not learn to read and write in early years
- Prejudice was too great to fight
- Could not beat the vicious cycle of poverty
- Could not speak and understand the English language
- Did not receive help or resources for learning disabilities
- Had to take care of other siblings or parents

So what is your next plan of action?

As the educational system continues to change, it is important for adult learners and professionals to find the right academic support and educational coaching to continue professional growth within their careers. Going back to earn your high school diploma, bachelor or master's degree is a sacrifice but once it is completed, many doors of opportunity can open and change a life forever. The hardest part of the process is walking into the continuing education admission's office.

Make a choice of instruction

Many schools, colleges and universities continue to offer **online learning** to instruct our students. <u>Is this really the best way to</u> <u>learn or is it simply more convenient</u> for students to sit at home and video conference with the teacher? I believe that *face-to-face* (and not "cyberface") really offers students a hands-on learning approach, ideals for collaborating together and daily structure to observe and respect different cultures and diversity. To me, that's why schools and colleges were built across the country so that students could go away to learn and come back to serve their communities. I challenge parents, coaches and administrators to take responsibility for how grades are earned online and to respectfully *monitor those grades authentically* each semester for permanent records in the online grade book. As a long-term educator, I know how easy it is to for someone else to do all the work in a math or English course for an enrolled student. In the long run, it will become even more apparent when written work does not quite match the student's assessed grade level. Genuine learning can always be demonstrated through proven levels of ability from kindergarten to college as well as continued job performance accountabilities long after in the real-world. The opposite end of this spectrum involves students who do not participate in the learning process at all: they don't turn in assignments, participate in class or show any type of engagement at all.

I remember taking the time to develop dozens of academic support plans and strategic solutions to many of my **2,500+ clients** since I started in 2005. When I see them all grown up or doing well professionally I realize it took me almost a lifetime to learn the complexities of our education system and offer solutions to help them navigate through it. **You can't just take the short cut to education.** The short cut ends up costing more money for tutoring and learning coaches. As a Learning Coach, I try to educate parents, students and athletes on the benefits to investing early in academic support intervention.

The report card continues to give a clear diagnosis but unfortunately many still insist on treating the symptoms instead of paying for the simple academic cure.

Finally, as I continue my educational quest to motivate, help struggling students and close the academic learning gap, use this book as

1. a plan of action

2. an educational resource to improve oral and written communication skills

3. an academic support supplement within your own home, school, college, university or facility forum.

From Kindergarten to Kollege in 10 Steps is 2022's "*best parent, student, athlete and professional's Quick Guide with ingenuity and insight for today's American Education System!*"

All my Best for Your Education Success,

Pamelyn Smythscott, M.Ed.
Education Consultant, Learning Coach and Certified "Big Pencil" Writing Specialist

Visit website for educational products, services and books at:
www.k-12learningcoach.com
Send e-mail inquiries and requests to: **gsclearningcoach@gmail.com**

Glossary of Educational Terms in Reading and Writing

Antagonist—character or force in conflict with main character in story or drama

Annotate—to write notes and explanations on the side margin of a book, article or literary work to understand subject material

Antonym—a word of opposite meaning (tall and short)

Apprenticeship—a novice who serves under professional leadership in exchange for learning experience and job skills earning monetary compensation

Author's purpose—reasons, thoughts and ideas for why we read and write

Autobiography—account of a person's life written by that person (usually told in first-person point of view)

Bias—personal or unreasoned judgment; prejudiced point of view

Biography—true account of a person's life told by someone else

Blending—using two or three consonants that make single sound (Ex: bl, thr, or sch)

Characters—people who take part in the action of the story, novel or drama

Claim—what a writer believes to be true stating proven or given facts, examples, statistics or cited information

Compare—when two things are similar (Ex: Red Delicious and Washington apples)

Consonants—letters in the alphabet that are <u>not</u> vowels (Ex: b,c,d)

Contrast—when two things are different (Ex: Granny Smith apple and a pineapple)

Cursive—act of joining letters together to make words in the form of penmanship that makes writing faster than printing or manuscript (Ex: writing or *writing*)

Cyberspace—way of using computers and devices to communicate through networks and applications technology

Decoding—basic understanding of each letter in the alphabet, the sounds they each make, and then blending them together to form words

Dialogue—written conversation between two or more characters in fiction or non-fiction

Dictation—reading words orally to be written down in order

Digraphs—a group of letters that make a single sound when used together (Ex: read or sing)

Diphthong—uses two vowels to make a one syllable sound (Ex. oil)

Diversity—showing difference among others; in backgrounds and cultures

Dystopian—fictional or imaginary place where people in community lead dehumanized or fearful lives; opposite of utopian

Encoding—stage of memorization for sight words (Ex. I, the, an) followed by using those letters and sounds as knowledge to write

English Language Arts—(also referred to as the acronym ELA) in school curriculums, educators teach four modes of language: the learning of reading, writing, listening and speaking to develop oral and written communication skills

Essay—brief composition on a certain topic that presents the views of the author in 350 words or more (types of essays include narrative, persuasive, expository, or personal)

Ethos—author uses a tactic of argument to show credibility or character

Evidence—information, examples or facts found in articles or stories that back up or support your claim

Figurative language—used in writing to help reader understand or show various emotions through use of literary terms (Ex: personification, hyperbole, simile and metaphor)

Genre—category or type of writing which includes descriptive, expository, narrative, persuasive, poetry and technical

HAC—Home Access Center is a program used to monitor academic grades and assignments from K-12; has password accessibility by parent and student

Handwriting—unique way of using written penmanship to communicate to others using cursive or print (manuscript)

Hyperbole—figure of speech using exaggeration for emphasis or humorous effect

Identification—how a writer shares a style, value or attitude toward a specific topic with an audience or reader

Imagery—words or phrases that appeal to the reader's five senses (see, taste, hear, feel and smell)

Individual Education Plan (IEP)—set by the state to meet and support a child's learning disability targets in trials at each grade level; signed and monitored by parent, principal and teacher from K-12

Inferences—reading between the lines to get main idea or gist based on what is found in the evidence or details in a story

Irony—contrast between appearance and reality; opposite from what it seems

Language—sounds in the oral form of communication

Leveled readers—a teacher strategy used in matching up a reader with a book on the same level

Literacy—ability and knowledge to read and write

Literary terms—personification, irony, symbol, imagery, foreshadowing, pun, paradox, allusion, simile, metaphor, onomatopoeia, setting, theme

Logos—author uses logic or reasoning to persuade reader to come to a certain realization

Manuscript—printed letters of the alphabet; opposite of cursive in which letters are joined together

Memoir—autobiographical writing; person recalls significant events in his or her life to share with others publically

Metaphor—figure of speech that compares two things that are unlike but have something in common; do not use like or as for comparison

Online learning—this is where learning or an education takes place over the internet; sometimes called "distance" learning since it is not in the classroom

Onomatopoeia—use of such words like Pow! Pop! Crunch!; the sound suggests their meaning

Pedagogy—the practice, methods, or concepts of teaching

Personification—figure of speech in which human qualities are attributed to an object, animal or idea (Ex: the sun crept in my room)

Phonemes—distinct sounds in beginning or ending of words

Plagiarism—taking other ideas, work or words as your own without giving credit to the source

Poetry—writing that reflects beauty or self-expression in the form or free verse, rhyming stanzas, sonnets or meters

Point of View (POV)—determining an angle or an opinion of an idea or situation; can come from the reader or author

Prior knowledge—memory of ideas, places and things experienced or already learned before

Procrastinate—to put off an important task or deadline until a later date or time

Prosody—the ability to read with expressiveness, smooth rhythm and emphasis; key factor in determining reading fluency

Protagonist—hero or main character in the story or narrative

Public Behavior System (PBS)—an organized network in place that monitors and redirects negative or poor behavior through consequences within a school community

Reading stamina—endurance for reading a number of pages over the course of hours or days

Remedial—raising overall competence of a core subject area through repeated instruction and practice strategies

Report Card—a grade assessment system in education to measure classroom performance in core subject areas

Rhetoric—used in writing using the art of persuasion to communicate; asking a question without providing an answer (rhetorical)

Rising action—builds suspense to a climax or turning point in a story or drama

Rubric—rated categories (1 lowest to 5 highest) for an assignment or project in which a grade is given for meeting the assigned guidelines

Satire—literally technique in which ideas or customs are ridiculed; used as witty, bitterly critical or mildly abrasive

Scaffolding—when educators break up learning concepts into chunks to move students along during instruction; sometimes called "chunking"

Sequence—order of events with dates or times in a story, article or event in reading

Sight words—knowing a word by heart or memorization; automatic recognition without decoding or sounding it out (Ex: the, an, like)

Simile—figure of speech that makes a comparison between two things using like or as (Ex: Her hurtful words cut like a sword)

Soliloquy—a speech in which a character speaks thoughts aloud

Speech—a presentation or public address to an audience; a refined art of talking

Student Education Plan (SEP)—set by the state to meet and support a student's learning disability at college; signed and monitored by educational advisory team

Support—finding evidence from a story or article in writing to back up response in writing

Syllables—pronouncing and breaking apart one, two, three or more sounds to form an entire word (Ex: sy/la/ble)

Syllabus—an outlined summary, description and expectations of a course, subject or program of study

Synonym—words that mean the same (hot, sweltering)

Synthesize—ability to combine several sources together to understand and explain the main point, focus or idea of the subject matter

Theme—main idea in a work of literature

Trace—to go back in your steps; (Ex: in literature, go back in story to find evidence)

Utopian—fictional or imagined society in which the people and community are perfect; opposite of dystopian

Vowels—letters of the alphabet that are <u>not</u> consonants (Ex: a,e,i,o,u)

Writing fluency—ability to write using both long and short sentences in paragraph format for literary purposes or specific genre responses

Writing traits—7 concepts used in the writing process to convey main ideas and messages; they are taught by The Learning Coach as the COWSVIP:

- Conventions (mechanical usage)
- Organization (introduction, body & conclusion)
- Word Choice (vocabulary)
- Sentence Fluency (sentence variety using questions, statements, commands, & declaratives)
- Voice (tone & style of message)
- Ideas (brainstorm & outline)
- Presentation (written paper, poster, PowerPoint, or project)

References

Common Core Standards. Www.doe.k12.de.us

Division of Aging. Www.hhs.gov

Division of Developmental Disabilities. Https://dhss.delaware.gov

Literacy Essentials & Reading Network. Www2.nefec.org

National Handwriting Association. Https://nha-handwriting.org.uk

Www.olmsteadrights.org

Www.psychologytoday.com

Www.scholastic.com

Volunteer survey group response for "Why Teachers Leave"

Volunteer survey group response for "What Clients Say"

Volunteer survey group response for "What Students Say"

Volunteer survey group response for "What Adult Learners Say"

The Learning Coach's School, College, University, Facilities & Contracts Since 2005

A. I. Dupont High	Mt. Pleasant High School
Appoquinomink High	M.O.T. Charter School
Avondale Academy, PA	Nativity School
Bear Library	Newark Charter High School
Caravel Academy	Newark High School
Christiana High School	Newark Free Library
Christina School District	New Castle Elementary School
DAPI School	Parents As Teachers
Delcastle Vo-Tech	Parkside Elementary School, PA
Delaware Futures Wilmington	Penn Cader Charter High
Delaware Military Academy	Penn Delco School District
*DTTC Upward Bound	Smyrna High School
Douglass Alternative School	Red Lion Charter
Downes Elementary School	Sarah Pyle Academy
Fairwinds Christian School	Serviam Girls Academy
Family Foundations Charter	Smyrna High School
Gallagher Elementary School	Southern Elementary School
Gunning Bedford Middle School	St. Georges Vo-Tech
Great Oaks Charter School	Thurgood Marshall Elementary
Hanby Middle School	Tower Hill School
Holy Angels School	Univ. of DE English Lang. Inst.
Home School Association	Univ. of DE Upward Bound
Howard Vo-Tech High School	Classic for Athletes
Kirkwood Library	Wienman & Associates Realty
McKean High School	William Penn High School
Meredith Middle School	Wilmington Christian School
Metropolitan Wilmington Urban League	Wilmington PAL Center
Middletown High School	

Get "The Learning Coach" at your next event.......... We've got what you need!

Visit our website at www.k-12Learningcoach.com

Send E-mail to gsclearningcoach@gmail.com or Call Us at 302-897-2991

Need a Guest Speaker?	Dramatic motivational speaking & book included for athletes, coaches, teams, facilities, conferences, orientations and organizations
Need Classes?	Small group (5, 10, 15) packages with book for students, parents, adult learners, professionals and English as Second Language
Need a Professional Development Coach or Trainer?	Fun built-in training activities that involves engaging hands-on lessons that include breakfast or lunch with your book & registration
Need Educational Consulting?	Academic, administrative & instructional support based on school, facility, college or university data
Need More Text Books?	Send request to Contact Information on website: **www.K-12learningcoach.com**
Need Really Big Pencils?	6-Foot Pencils personally hand- crafted! Great marketing tool for schools, business lobby displays, classrooms, special events, student awards, kids' rooms, college dorms, offices and writing centers.

***Book pre-order is required for staff and group participation**

What Parents and Clients Say About The Learning Coach

(Names are protected & statements have been reconstructed for their privacy)

Joy's daughter was in Grade 4 and had trouble with reading in special education so they called The Learning Coach to help with her IEP in speech, reading, writing and education strategies in the class room. After working with them for two years, her daughter moved up one grade level. Joy is now supported at the parent teacher meetings and understands her child's learning disabilities.

Debbie's son benefitted from The Learning Coach during his 8th and 9th grade year. Ms. Scott identified his strengths and weaknesses and recommended more challenging material through intensified instruction. Her son progressed from "on-level" work and by his Senior year had completed both Honors and AP English classes. He now studies in Europe to further his education.

Monique's goal was working her way up to a better paying job, but her writing, grammar and vocabulary skills needed help. As she pursued her Associate's degree, The Learning Coach helped her with writing assignments. She also called us to help with the job interview preparation. Monique got the new job and still calls The Learning Coach when she needs academic and business coaching.

Rolanda's son was in Grade 9 and needed to improve his handwriting. Though she was convinced that he would grow out of it, she called The Learning Coach for a free consultation. Shortly after, they started handwriting strategies for legibility, sentence structure and he soon improved one grade level after 8 months. Rolanda realized that the time spent in tutoring was worth the time and commitment to get the academic help her son really needed before it was too late.

Both Wendy's two daughters are now in college and tutored with The Learning Coach since they were in elementary for reading and writing. When Wendy lost her job, Ms. Scott came to their house and never missed a session to keep academic momentum. Wendy believes that the service is trusted and her kids are a product of academic support that works.

Yenaly's 8th grader didn't like school and wouldn't complete classwork or homework. Her grades were failing and writing was not legible. Yenaly was referred to The Learning Coach to help but when her daughter didn't show any motivation, Ms. Scott kindly returned her money and told them that when they were ready, she would be happy to start the service. Now Yenaly's daughter is failing Grade 10 and she has called again. This time her daughter pays with her own money for tutoring through her part-time job and sees the value of academic support to graduate.

Margaret and her husband realized that their daughter in Grade 3 struggled with meeting Common Core Standards mastery in writing. With busy schedules, it was hard for them to get her to tutoring sessions but they began to manage. When they saw the progress their daughter was making after one year with The Learning Coach, they were proud of the progress on her report card and was glad they made the call.

Chris and Alex's daughter in Grade 11 failed Drivers Education and English. They knew of only one person to call for academic support. After one year with The Learning Coach, their daughter got back on track and she finally passed Drivers Ed and earned a B in English. Soon they began to tell other parents who believed that tutoring was a waste of money an important message: If you know your child has been struggling, *yesterday* was the time to put in the effort to invest in your child's future.

Rev. Rick brought his Grade 9 daughter, who was failing two subjects, reluctantly to tutoring with The Learning Coach. After a few sessions, Ms. Scott sensed that they had not bought in to the value of tutoring and kindly returned their money. Rev. Rick shared that he should have intervened in middle school and did not seek the academic support his daughter really needed. He respected Ms. Scott's keen insight for his daughter's academic learning plan that was well on target during the initial consultation.

What Students and Athletes Say About The Learning Coach

Ben sat the bench during his junior year basketball season and needed to keep his promised athletic scholarship for next year. There was nothing his coach could do and his parents were very upset. After working with The Learning Coach for a whole school year, his academic habits changed and he made the team in the fall. Now a Senior, Ben is very proud of his 2.3 G.P.A. which is a C but he worked hard to bring it up from a 1.3 (F).

Isu was in Grade 12, hung out with the wrong crowds and got suspended from the football team. He needed help in keeping up his grades so his parents called The Learning Coach. Ms. Scott worked with him during the suspension to maintain his academics and complete assignments. Isu realized that even by association, anyone can get in trouble. He also knew that he tutored with Ms. Scott in elementary and her academic support services still worked.

Myeshia got accepted into the University but did not have the academics to maintain the required 2.5 G.P.A. She was failing all her English classes and didn't bother to attend the others. After her parents could no longer afford to pay for her tutoring sessions with The Learning Coach, she had to start paying for them with her part-time job. That's when she learned the value of hard earned money and really respected her parents now for making her do this on her my own.

Writing was not Rudy's thing—well so was reading and just getting through high school. He began working with The Learning Coach for over a year to get ready for college. He admits to messing around but now that he was actually going to graduate, he understood now why his parents and tennis coach were so hard on him. Rudy learned how to be a better writer and test taker with the tutoring sessions.

Teen mom Annakia had dyslexia and no one ever knew it in high school. She struggled with everything from English to Science and failed almost everything because she couldn't read it—everything appeared backwards. After graduation, she called The Learning Coach because she needed help finding a job, learning to drive and learning business skills to go back to college. Annakia finally invested in herself and has a good paying job.

Sewell's mom wanted him to go to college but it just wasn't for him. He wanted to work after graduation. With his learning disabilities, he barely made it out of high school. He tried Community College but he skipped half the time because writing and English was hard. He tutored with The Learning Coach in elementary and middle school. Sewell finally graduated high school and that made his mom happy. Now he works and makes more money than his mom and this makes him happy.

Jack plays sports at a private school all year, every day, and through all seasons. As a freshman, he's good at every sport. Only problem is that his grades are low and he knows he needs a tutor. He worked with The Learning Coach before but his practice schedule kept getting in the way of attending tutoring sessions. Ms. Scott reasoned that if he puts this much effort into sports, that same effort should go into his academic studies. Not liking the looks of his last few report card, Jack realizes that tutor grown- ups are usually right.

After taking an English course at the Community College, Lexie knew her writing and speaking skills were unpolished. She kept putting it off in high school and putting it off as she got better positions at work. It soon showed up in the college course when she had to do an oral presentation and complete written assignments. The Learning Coach helped her invest in herself and Lexie has learned to be more confident speaking in front of others at work.

Angelo's dad pushed him while he was a Senior in high school to get tutoring. He knew he wasn't a good writer, but he still dreamed of attending a good university film school. The Learning Coach prepared him for leaving home and being the first-generation to graduate. He smiles about it now but was sad back then when his dad worked three jobs to make things better for him. Angelo is still in college because he wants to make his dad proud of him.

What Adult Learners Say About The Learning Coach

(Names are protected & statements have been reconstructed for their privacy)

Writing a book was something Carol wanted to do, but didn't have the stamina or will power to finish. Instead she knew she needed business writing skill strategies from The Learning Coach. After several months of executive sessions, she could confidently compete in her department with corporate staff. Carol also began putting the pieces together to write her own memoir for publication.

Dynah believed that investing in herself was pretty simple: if you can afford gourmet coffee every day for a year, you can afford executive coaching for 6-8 weeks to improve your communication skills and business presence.

Nikka held supervisor roles for years but didn't feel confident about her limited vocabulary around her staff. She knew she needed to work on it but kept putting it off. When a job opened up for her to move up, she called The Learning Coach. She admits she was scared to call at first, but she realized that FEAR really means False Evidence Appearing Real. She is now the head of an executive team.

Larrilyn's son was receiving academic support from The Learning Coach and one day after their session, she asked for private executive coaching for herself. Just as her son learned academic concepts and strategies to perform better in his classroom, she learned how to be a better oral presenter at work. Speaking in front of others still makes her nervous, but she still relies on oral presentation strategies to combat those fears.

Hector's transition to the U.S from Mexico was a hard transition with his learning disabilities and broken English but he wanted more for his family. He worked three jobs to pay for the coaching sessions and practiced speaking and listening skills with The Learning Coach. Now, people understand what he says and he has gained more confidence in his vocabulary.

As an author, Quillen wanted the skills to learn how to interact in person with his readership. After he called the Learning Coach, he discovered so much about himself in about six sessions. He began to book more community engagements and signed books with confidence. He also gained insight that his next handshake could lead into even more book marketing opportunities.

Pattricia came to The Learning Coach for help in starting a business. There were so many things that she didn't know but was willing to make the first step. The Learning Coach analyzed her skills and experience to match the right service to offer: her new non-profit organization fit perfectly into the local community.

Going back to school was something Mitch, now retired, never thought he could do after being out 30 years. His vocabulary and reading skills were low and he thought he was too old. After pep talks, sessions and motivational conversations with The Learning Coach, he passed the college course with a "B" and confidently registered for another session.

When Paris' husband got laid off from work, she stopped going to her executive coaching sessions with The Learning Coach to improve her business skills. Though finances were tough, she didn't want to quit in the middle and wanted to get promoted at work. She stepped out on faith to keep up sessions and Ms. Scott worked out payment arrangements. Paris believes that when you invest in something purposeful for yourself, the right people will come along to help you.

Kaleb kept seeing his kids and friends graduate college which made him realize that he needed to further his education, too. Although he dropped out of high school, Ms. Scott helped him study and pass the GED certificate program. When his academic skills in reading and writing improved, he got a better paying job two weeks later.

Pastor Thomas wrote several books but with his busy schedule he really needed someone to help him with time management and stay on top of publishing deadlines. He believes that you should be careful in what you pray for: The Learning Coach was a Godsend to him and his congregation.

THE LEARNING COACH, LLC

"We help students and athletes get better grades."

Use the chart below to check reading and writing skills for academic success!

Grades K-5 Elementary	Grades 6-8 Middle School	Grades 9-12 High School	Kollege & Career Readiness
• Handwriting • Phonetics • Vowel Sounds • RDG on grade level • Sentence Structure • Paragraphs • Spelling • RDG fluency • Vocabulary	• Writing legibility • RDG on grade level • 7 Writing Traits • Transitions • Main Idea • Paragraphs • Vocabulary • Critical Thinking • Research • Test Taking Strategies • Digital Literacy Skills	• Writing legibility • RDG on grade level • 7 Writing Traits • Transitions • Thesis • Main Idea • Paragraphs • Vocabulary • Proofreading & Editing • Group Presentation • Critical Thinking • Research • Test Taking Strategies • Time Management • PSAT/SAT Prep • College Essays • Digital Literacy Skills	• Writing legibility • Response to text • Critical Thinking in RDG & WTNG • Thesis • Restated thesis • Narratives • Persuasion • Analysis • Research • Vocabulary • 7 Writing Traits • Proofreading & Editing • Oral Presentation • Study Skills • Time Management • RDG, WTG & MTH Placement • Communication Skills • Digital Literacy Skills

2019
This is a Learning Coach Presentation
www.K-12LearnigCoach.com

NOTES

NOTES

NOTES

NOTES

NOTES

NOTES

NOTES

NOTES

NOTES

NOTES

NOTES

NOTES

NOTES

NOTES

NOTES